INSPIRED DESIGN

INSPIRED DESIGN

THE 100 MOST IMPORTANT INTERIOR DESIGNERS OF THE PAST 100 YEARS

JENNIFER BOLES

A STEPHEN DRUCKER BOOK

VENDOME

NEW YORK · LONDON

CONTENTS

THE GLOBALISTS

THE GRANDEES

LIKE NO OTHER

GONE TOO SOON

MAKING THEIR MARK

INTRODUCTION

As anyone who has read my blog can attest, my world revolves around floral chintzes and animal prints, porcelains and Parsons tables, and the likes of David Hicks and Dorothy Draper. Over the last decade, via the pages of thepeakofchic.com, I have celebrated the history of decorating and decorators (or interior designers, if you prefer) of all stripes: great lady decorators and contemporary designers; American, English, French, and even Russian ones. So high is my regard for the profession that I have devoted entire articles to interior designers from the past whom no one seems to remember anymore. Does the name Pierre Dutel ring a bell?

To those of you who are included in this book, congratulations. And to those who are not, I want to salute you too. Everyone involved in producing this book shares my respect for every designer, which is why we took the responsibility of selecting the one hundred featured here very seriously. We spent many hours considering people past and present, concentrating on their very specific contributions to the design profession. Decisions were made neither hastily nor arbitrarily, while the occasional disagreements were always met with cool heads and open minds. I contacted editors of decorating magazines, hoping to get the biggest possible perspective; you'll find their opinions on the past century's most important designers on these pages. And in an effort to avoid any semblance of favoritism, we even opened up the floor to public discussion using a very twenty-first-century tool: social media. The team at Kravet, whose centennial anniversary inspired this book; my editor, Stephen Drucker; and I all took to Facebook and Instagram, asking individuals to name the most important designers of the last century. We received hundreds of replies, all of which were factored into our list. If you are one who answered us, thank you, because your response helped shape this book.

All lists are ambitious, cheeky, and sometimes confounding. They're also fun, provocative, and great starting points for important discussions. Some of the designers featured on these pages may seem obvious choices, while others will surprise you. You may disagree with who did, or did not, make our list. Some of my own favorite designers, those I would hire to decorate my own home, are in fact missing. But what can be said of all one hundred is that in some shape or form, they influenced the course of design and made a lasting impression. Perhaps they legitimized their profession in its early days, or maybe they introduced a new way of thinking or working. Some created interiors of such beauty and acclaim, we're still talking about them today. That, in the end, is the truest test.

For the record, my choice for the most important designer of the past century is Albert Hadley. Although he might have continued what his predecessor and friend Billy Baldwin started decades prior, it was Hadley who guaranteed the longevity of classic American decorating by successfully ushering it into the twenty-first century. The creator of some truly remarkable interiors—in numbers rivaling those of any other designer—Hadley managed to imbue his rooms with a sense of the past updated by a modern spirit. The result was a body of work that remains timeless and relevant. Will the red-lacquered library Hadley created for Brooke Astor ever look dated? I sincerely doubt it.

STEPHEN DRUCKER
Editor in Chief, *House Beautiful* (2005–2010)

There is such an absurd overemphasis on decorating these days.
The two designers I most admire reflect my wish to restore some
balance and sanity to the design world.

For me everything begins with Billy Baldwin. Not because he was
charming; the one time I called my idol, he told me to leave him alone and
hung up on me. But because *Billy Baldwin Decorates* is the best book ever
on the subject, with a healthy, humble perspective on what matters and
what doesn't; and because Baldwin, following his own advice, came closer
than anybody to creating timeless rooms—a virtually impossible feat.

From Billy Baldwin I see a straight line to Tom Scheerer today. Like
Baldwin, Scheerer has perfect pitch for what's appropriate; he never lets a
room—or a client—become too grand for its own good. Also like Baldwin,
Scheerer has some tricks he uses in almost every project. Sometimes
I hear someone say, "Can't he do something new?" They're totally missing
the point. The mark of experience and self-confidence is not chasing
novelty for novelty's sake. I wish there were more designers like him today.

AMY ASTLEY
Editor in Chief, *Architectural Digest* (2016–)

Pierre Yovanovitch is very much "right now"—influential, directional, a
talent that the whole design world is watching. But he also has a classical
viewpoint that ensures longevity, conjuring up minimalist interiors that
have warmth, softness, and a sense of humor. His rooms are lean but not
undernourished, full of plump shapes and soulful textures (he handles
dramatically veined marble and earthy wood elements better than
anyone), and dosed with subtle colors. There's also always a vintage touch
that lets you know how much he appreciates the history of design at the
same time he's looking into the future.

NEWELL TURNER
Editor in Chief, Hearst Design Group (2012–)

I'm a huge fan of the California decorators John Dickinson and Michael Taylor. Their careers spanned roughly the same time, from the '50s to the early '80s, but I don't think they were friends, much less shared any sense of camaraderie in design. Yet their work has had a powerful influence on American style. Their common ground? A sense of European elegance evolved via the East Coast, but infused with a Zen-like approach to color, materials, and furniture placement that came directly across the Pacific.

CLINTON SMITH
Editor in Chief, *Veranda* (2013–)

There are so many unsung interior designers with unrivaled taste who imparted style and education to clients who purposefully lived beyond the confines of New York and Los Angeles. Think of Otto Zenke's new classicism in 1960s North Carolina, John Astin Perkins's riotous mix of '70s color and pattern in Dallas, Babs Watkins's Swedish sensibility in oil-fueled Houston in the 1980s; Charles Faudree's French Country taste in Tulsa in the '90s and early aughts, and, from the 1930s on, Porter & Porter and Edith Hills's reign over Atlanta society. They're just a few of the star twentieth-century talents who left an indelible mark on beauty, taste, and lasting design in their respective communities—and beyond.

MARIAN McEVOY
Editor in Chief, *Elle Decor* (1991–2000), *House Beautiful* (2000–2002)

Jacques Grange has been my interior design hero for over forty years. A Jacques Grange room is like the man himself—haute European, confident, and multifaceted. Like a great fine artist, Grange can break all the rules and still make it work. What a talent.

SOPHIE DONELSON
Editor in Chief, *House Beautiful* (2015–)

You can't see Tony Baratta's work and not feel a wave of happiness wash over you—and immediately question why your own home is so square. Baratta and his late partner, Bill Diamond, commissioned the finest craftspeople in America, from fiber artists to faux painters, and together they had the most fun in the world. Call his rooms unconventional—and thank god.

LISA NEWSOM
Editor in Chief, *Veranda* (1987–2010)

The California style was created by Michael Taylor. Large boulders, stone, and natural wood were his foundation. Using trees and plants, Taylor brought the outside in—something we are still doing today. Denouncing clutter, he once said, " When you take something out, you must increase the size of what is left." It was Cecil Beaton who gave him his greatest compliment. Beaton once asked a prominent editor, "How is the best decorator in America doing?" She answered, naming several design greats. Beaton retorted, "No, No, I mean Michael Taylor. He's the innovative one, the original!"

MICHAEL BOODRO
Editor in Chief, *Elle Decor* (2010–2017)

Theirs was a world in which you could never be too rich or too thin—or have too much majolica. For Robert Denning and Vincent Fourcade, decorating was a matter of balance, but in their case that meant piling it on until just short of a total collapse, with luxury battling abundance to a precise, precarious, and ravishing standstill. All of history seemed to come together in a grand, well-mannered bacchanalia. Yet excess was always tempered by expertise, and chaos was kept at bay by connoisseurship. It was all dazzling, but never de trop.

WHITNEY ROBINSON
Editor in Chief, *Elle Decor* (2017–)

Bunny Williams is the Meryl Streep of the interior design world. Or is it Linda Evangelista? Perhaps no other living designer is more beloved or has been awarded more honors, and for good reason. Her signature interiors are a blend of old-world English collected comfort—with an American sensibility and wallet. But for Bunny, cozy isn't enough. She thinks about how a house is sited, how the art is curated, how the garden is planted, and most important, how her clients really live and entertain. I remember the first interior of hers that I shot, on what was then the most expensive piece of real estate ever sold in the Hamptons. It was pure Bunny, fabulous yet familiar. I vowed when I made my first $100 million to call her.

NANCY NOVOGROD
Editor in Chief, *HG* (1988–1993)

It was the fall of 1987, the heyday of the English country house style in U.S. interiors, and chintz was reigning supreme. I was presented with a copy of an Oklahoma magazine featuring an interior by a talented young designer who had recently landed in New York. There were lots of imaginative decorative elements—columns, busts, globes, some of which now sound like pure cliché, but then seemed fresh—and all was on a rather comfortable human scale. The color palette was also refreshing: greige, in an age of red cabbage roses. Thus began my romance with Stephen Sills and his former longtime partner, James Huniford, aka Ford. During my five years as editor in chief of *HG*, I published scores of projects by Sills Huniford—and in every single case, it felt a bit like Christmas when I received scouting shots of a new project.

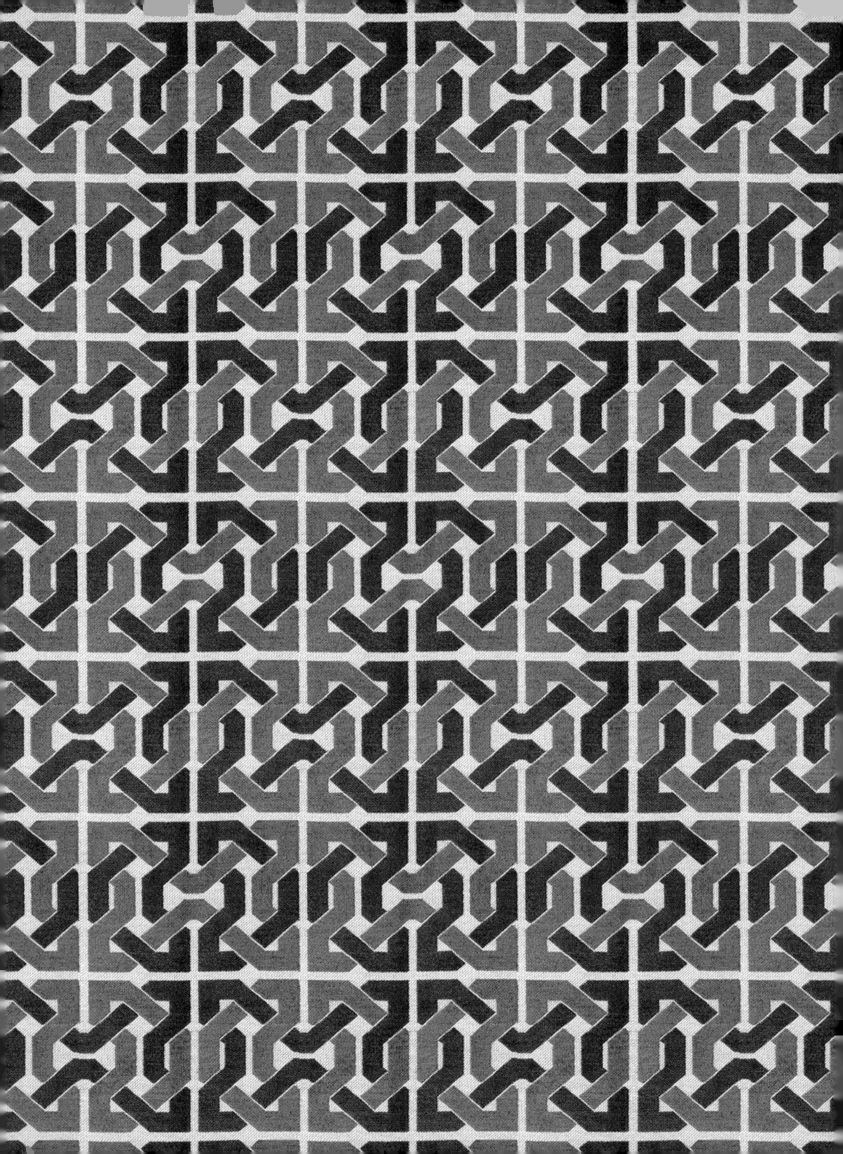

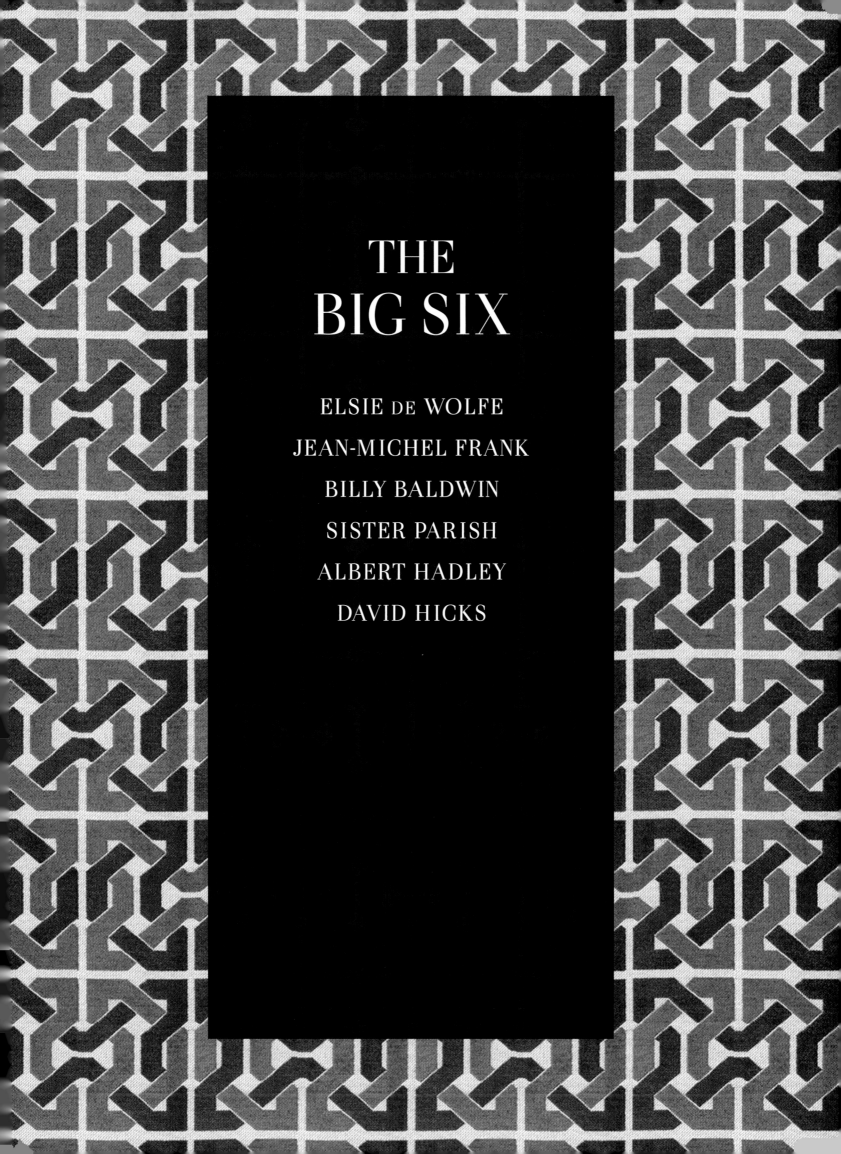

THE
BIG SIX

ELSIE DE WOLFE

JEAN-MICHEL FRANK

BILLY BALDWIN

SISTER PARISH

ALBERT HADLEY

DAVID HICKS

1 | Elsie de Wolfe

1865–1950

"I believe in plenty of optimism and white paint."

Late Victorian decorating might have shown a dearth of taste, but it nonetheless managed to produce one positive: Elsie de Wolfe, who is often called the first modern professional decorator. She was a self-described rebel in an ugly world who made beauty her mission. **De Wolfe banished her era's gloom and bric-a-brac mania in favor of "simplicity, suitability, and proportion"**—the concept that became the cornerstone of twentieth-century design. Using as her pulpit her now-legendary 1913 decorating guide, *The House in Good Taste,* de Wolfe preached the virtues of pale color schemes, floral chintzes, painted woodwork, and slender French furniture, all of which not only introduced lightness and femininity to interiors previously starved of both, but also restored dignity to American design.

One of her earliest commissions was possibly her most influential: the interiors of the Colony Club, the exclusive Manhattan women's club, where she popularized the use of painted trellis as an indoor wall-covering—an insistently cheerful motif that has yet to wane a century later. But her most memorable decorating scheme was also her most personal: her beloved home in Versailles, Villa Trianon. Site of her legendary 1938 Circus Ball, the modish house helped to propel the Francophile decorator into the ranks of café society, yet another achievement in a profession once associated with tradesmen.

While some of her later novelties, like her penchant for blue hair, never quite caught on, others, especially animal-print carpeting and mirrored walls, signal a particular breed of sophistication and worldliness to this day, and have consolidated Wolfe's reputation as the grande dame of modern decorating.

Opposite By 1941, when Horst P. Horst photographed her in this dramatic setting, Elsie de Wolfe had left her Victorian childhood far behind, and was a full-fledged member of European café society. **Above** For theatrical agent Elisabeth Marbury's Sutton Place home, de Wolfe devised a feminine sitting room employing many of her early signature decorations: French furniture, sprightly floral patterns, and leopard-print upholstery. **Overleaf** In the 1930s, when de Wolfe decorated a Park Avenue apartment for the actress Hope Hampton, her style was overtly glamorous, with mirror and animal prints leading the way.

2 | Jean-Michel Frank
1895–1941

"Two things seem equally impossible to me: to live in a modern house where it would be a shock to walls and furniture if a Louis XV clock were put on the mantel, or to furnish a period room to such perfection that you really wonder where you will hide the telephone."

Above A central figure in Paris artistic circles of the 1920s and '30s, Jean-Michel Frank frequently collaborated with the era's greatest figures, including Alberto Giacometti, Emilio Terry, and Christian Bérard. **Opposite** With its parchment-lined walls and straw marquetry furniture, Charles and Marie-Laure de Noailles's smoking room in their Paris residence on place des États-Unis was Frank's masterpiece. **Overleaf** Frank's luxurious form of modernism appealed to Nelson A. Rockefeller, whose Fifth Avenue living room was a departure for the designer, less austere and more colorful. The room's furnishings were selected with Rockefeller's collection of Matisse paintings in mind.

Paris was the capital of artistic achievement in the 1920s. Pablo Picasso, Jean Cocteau, F. Scott Fitzgerald, Gertrude Stein . . . and **Jean-Michel Frank, who forged a new modern decorative style that combined two qualities previously considered contradictory: simplicity and luxury.**

Frank's style, an exercise in elimination, stripped interiors of unnecessary ornament, the resulting sparseness requiring furnishings of unimpeachable quality. Furniture—what there was of it—was distilled to its essence, pure of line and shape. Color was monastic, with shades of cream and beige barely registering. Texture was everything. Sanded oak and coarse cotton textiles, not traditionally associated with high-end decorating, were used with sumptuous parchment, shagreen, straw marquetry, and Hermès leather applied to tables, cabinets, and often walls.

Only the most refined eye could appreciate rooms this subtle, and Frank's work appealed to the most forward-thinking members of the social elite, who could afford his expensive brand of simplicity. His greatest patrons were Charles and Marie-Laure de Noailles, for whom the designer created a smoking room lavished with parchment and mica at One place des États-Unis in Paris; it might be the most famous modern room of the twentieth century. But there was also Frank's Fifth Avenue living room for Nelson A. Rockefeller, which became a defining moment in America's march to modernism. Amplifying Frank's reputation were his furniture designs, especially his boxy upholstery and geometric lamps, which proved popular with other innovative decorators, especially Frances Elkins.

Frank came of age in a golden moment, but it was to be short-lived. He was Jewish and fled his beloved France ahead of the Occupation and deportations. He moved first to Buenos Aires, and then to New York City, but could not see his own future; he committed suicide in Manhattan, only forty-six years old. His life was brief, but it would be hard to find a decorator whose rooms are more admired, whose furniture has been more copied, and who has challenged us more to ponder the real meaning of luxury.

3 | Billy Baldwin
1903–1983

> "I'm against the all-English house or the all-French house or the all-Spanish house—any of these must be translated into terms that suit the American Way for the America today."

Before World War II it was the Europeans who influenced American decorating, but by the 1950s, it was a home-grown talent defining American design: Billy Baldwin. A Southerner who was short of stature but made an outsize impression, Baldwin ventured to New York City in 1935, training with the legendary Ruby Ross Wood before founding his own firm. Quickly establishing himself as both a gifted decorator and a man-about-town, Baldwin assembled a glittering clientele, which included Cole Porter, Babe Paley, Jacqueline Kennedy Onassis, and the Paul Mellons. Among his unforgettable projects were the tented Kenneth hair salon, the beehive of New York society in the Jet Set era; one of the world's great trophy houses, La Fiorentina, for the Harding Lawrences; and perhaps most notably, Diana Vreeland's red "garden in hell" living room on Park Avenue.

What set Baldwin's style apart was a feeling of "Americanness." He reveled in comfort and simplicity. His cotton fabrics, signature upholstery like the St. Thomas sofa, and affection for clear, strong colors—he said he did not believe in starting out half dead—spoke to the modern, relaxed atmosphere of post–World War II America, while contemporary art, lacquered surfaces, and gleaming brass accents supplied the polish that his worldly clients required. **Under Baldwin's influence, high society, which once perched daintily on silk-covered fauteuils, began lazing on cotton-covered ottomans and slipper chairs.**

He was not an easy man. It was said that "his sting was deep." He hated the self-aggrandizing term "interior designer," preferring the more straightforward "decorator." He did not mince his opinions: "The word that almost makes me throw up is satin. Damask makes me throw up."

No doubt the purest example of his vision was his own final apartment in Manhattan, which remains a pivotal moment in the history of American style. It was just one room, but its lacquered chocolate-brown walls, off-white cotton upholstery, rattan tables, and brass étagère bookshelves proved a groundbreaking combination that set the standard for modern American design. What greater compliment is there than to say this apartment looks every bit as good today as it did fifty years ago?

Left A cheerleader for humble cotton, Baldwin custom-designed his most recognizable fabric for the Manhattan living room of Woodson Taulbee, whose Matisse drawing, hung above the sofa, inspired the print. **Opposite** "You almost feel as if you're walking on a bridge, so airy and full of light is the living room" was how Baldwin described La Fiorentina, the quintessential French Riviera getaway of the Harding Lawrences. (To see Roderick Cameron's version of La Fiorentina, turn to pages 98–99.) **Overleaf** Baldwin's one-room Manhattan apartment is still hugely influential due to its mix of chocolate-brown-lacquered walls, gleaming brass bookcases, and slipcovered seating, including his signature slipper chairs.

Of those legendary brass bookcases, originally designed for Cole Porter's residence at the Waldorf Towers, Baldwin said, "Very soon after the photographs of the apartment were published, the bookcases began appearing everywhere."

4 Sister Parish
1910–1994

> "If my Undecorated Look has meant rooms that
> are personal, comfortable, friendly, and gay,
> I feel I have accomplished a great deal."

Despite lacking a formal design education, Mrs. Henry "Sister" Parish II arrived at decorating already ably equipped. Bearing the taste and the confidence of her patrician background, **Parish purveyed an aesthetic— traditional, well-bred, and never too new-looking— that became the defining style of America's old guard.** Championing Americanness, her work was the WASP-y definition of town-and-country chic.

After an early solo success decorating the private rooms of the Kennedy White House, Parish famously partnered with Albert Hadley—the traditional yin to his modern yang—and went on to decorate for the social elite, including the Paleys, the Whitneys, and the Engelhards. Willful and cantankerous, Parish had strong opinions about decorating, but, like her partner, somehow in the end always conceived interiors that reflected the personalities of her clients. The hallmark of a Parish-Hadley room was that it lacked a discernible one.

Never one to make a showy statement—in the 1930s, she used humble mattress ticking for her living room curtains, a gesture unheard of at that time—Parish worked hard to create that lack of pretension, especially in the country. There, Parish indulged in her favorite furnishings, which represented the best of American crafts: rag rugs, quilts, painted furniture, baskets, and decoupage. Her own house in Dark Harbor, Maine, where she summered her entire life, is a classic example of American country style.

In city homes she took a more polished approach, with superb porcelains and antiques appropriate for cosmopolitan living, though she had a gift for knocking down even these rooms with chintzes and baskets rather than damasks and Sèvres. In one famous story, an antique was delivered and placed between two windows, though it was clearly too large for that spot. The upset client was taught a lesson in the Parish way: "You don't want it to look like you bought it to go there."

Opposite Upper-crust and crusty, Parish, seen here in her office in the 1970s, rarely decorated beyond her social milieu. **Left** The guest bedroom of Parish's beloved Dark Harbor, Maine, home, the nexus of everything she loved: rag rugs, baskets, chintz, and decoupage. **Overleaf** No one handled traditional American decorations better than Sister Parish, as seen in her design for the Whitney family's horse farm in Saratoga, New York. "I'm not an authority," said Parish. "It's just that I have a knack." **Pages 20–21** In the early 1970s, Parish allowed Hadley to redecorate her New York City living room with contemporary cotton prints and aubergine- lacquered walls. Old habits die hard; within a short time, she abandoned the scheme for her old guard favorites.

5 | Albert Hadley
1920–2012

> "I think we all want to do something radical and different, but the temptation should be overcome."

The heir to Billy Baldwin, Tennessee-bred Albert Hadley was, like his predecessor, both a traditionalist and a modernist. He worked in no one style. He was as comfortable decorating a nineteenth-century Louisiana plantation as he was a twentieth-century high-rise in Manhattan. But **Hadley's particular form of genius was his ability to seamlessly negotiate a compromise between the old and the new**, a skill that proved especially valuable when working with Sister Parish, his more conservative partner at their design firm, Parish-Hadley Associates.

He was above all an editor. Parish would put in, he would take out. Their traditional interiors always felt fresh, never old-fashioned, thanks to his judicious hand with adventurous accents and his perfect pitch for space and architectural effects. A graphic-patterned cotton fabric, sometimes of his own design; a sparkling finish, such as the oxblood-lacquered walls of Brooke Astor's library, one of Hadley's masterpieces; or architecture-blurring elements, such as mirrored baseboards and shimmery tea-papered ceilings—they would all work to update a room's more conventional features, moving them toward the future and away from the past. Yet in a Hadley-designed house, periods and styles mixed so naturally one could never be sure he had actually been there.

Having been taken under the wing of the likes of Baldwin, Van Day Truex, and onetime boss Eleanor McMillen Brown after arriving in New York in 1947, Hadley famously continued this tradition of mentorship throughout his life. Being invited to his timeless Manhattan apartment, and being served a stiff drink with a small bowl of potato chips by Hadley in his signature turtleneck, cigarette in hand, was a rite of passage for New York decorators. With illustrious alumni like Bunny Williams, Brian McCarthy, David Easton, Mariette Himes Gomez, and Thom Filicia—the list goes on and on—Parish-Hadley proved to be the ultimate design school, earning Hadley the reputation as the dean of American decorating.

Opposite Wearing his uniform of turtleneck and wool pants, and standing in his glossy red hallway, Hadley often greeted young designers in his apartment. The first stop was the grog tray in his kitchen.
Left Hadley considered his work on the Far Hills, New Jersey home of Mrs. Nancy "Princess" Pyne, whose living room is seen here, among his favorite. "There was no one like Albert Hadley," said Pyne. "God, he had taste."
Overleaf The defining room of Hadley's career, Brooke Astor's library, with its sang-de-boeuf enameled walls, brass trim, and Brunschwig & Fils La Portugaise fabric, was a high-water mark in late twentieth-century American design.

6 | David Hicks

1929–1998

"I don't really like people very much.
They bore me. I like objects."

Opposite David Hicks never lacked in confidence, once declaring,
"My favorite decorator is myself." Above Quintessential Hicks, this
gutsy English study was decorated in the mid-1960s.
Overleaf Believing "the more shades of a particular color you put
together the better the result will be," Hicks introduced heart-
racing reds, purples, and pinks into the Long Room at Britwell,
his house in Oxfordshire, England. The room became a sensation.
Page 30 Bedrooms were a particular forte of Hicks, who started
a fad for canopy beds that were in name only; the bed canopy
and hangings were attached directly to the ceiling rather than
supported by bedposts. Page 31 One of Hicks's most famous
rooms, this London drawing room, designed in 1964 for the
Hon. Anthony Samuel, featured green velvet walls and a collection
of pre-Colombian gold displayed in Hicks's inimitable style.

If the decorating world today sometimes seems awash in
hexagons and chevrons, it is David Hicks we have to thank.

Success was inevitable for this Englishman. Confidence
defined him. He looked like James Bond. He married brilliantly, to Pamela Mountbatten, the daughter of India's last
viceroy and a member of one of England's most illustrious
families, placing him at the highest levels of society and
culture in the 1960s and 1970s, when England ruled the
style world. There was no design David Hicks felt he could
not improve: fabrics, carpets, sheets, jumbo-jet interiors,
neckties.

But he not only had the confidence, he also had the talent. Think back to the pell-mell days of sixties and seventies
design, of brash colors and pattern spinning out of control.
Not so for Hicks, who indulged in the brazen fashions of the
day while managing to do what few others could: he tamed
them. With the self-assured Hicks in charge, even the most
shocking shades of crimson, magenta, and orange found
equilibrium. He could mix the boldest patterns, especially
his graphic-print carpets, which Billy Baldwin claimed
"revolutionized the floors of the world," and somehow the
clashing designs were neutralized. His intense discipline
could be felt, never more so than when arranging objects
in one of his celebrated "tablescapes." **Hicks left us with
interiors so well-constructed they remain master classes in balance and discipline.**

As remarkable as Hicks's talent was his uncanny ability
to anticipate the way forward in design, which he articu-
lated in a series of sometimes self-aggrandizing books. His
rooms felt thrillingly modern, but never aggressively so.
His pared-down upholstery and cotton fabrics predicted
our future of casual living, while his regard for classic
shapes and antiques preserved continuity with the past.
Today this middle ground, neither wholly traditional nor
contemporary, is where most interior design resides, but
no doubt about it, David Hicks got there first.

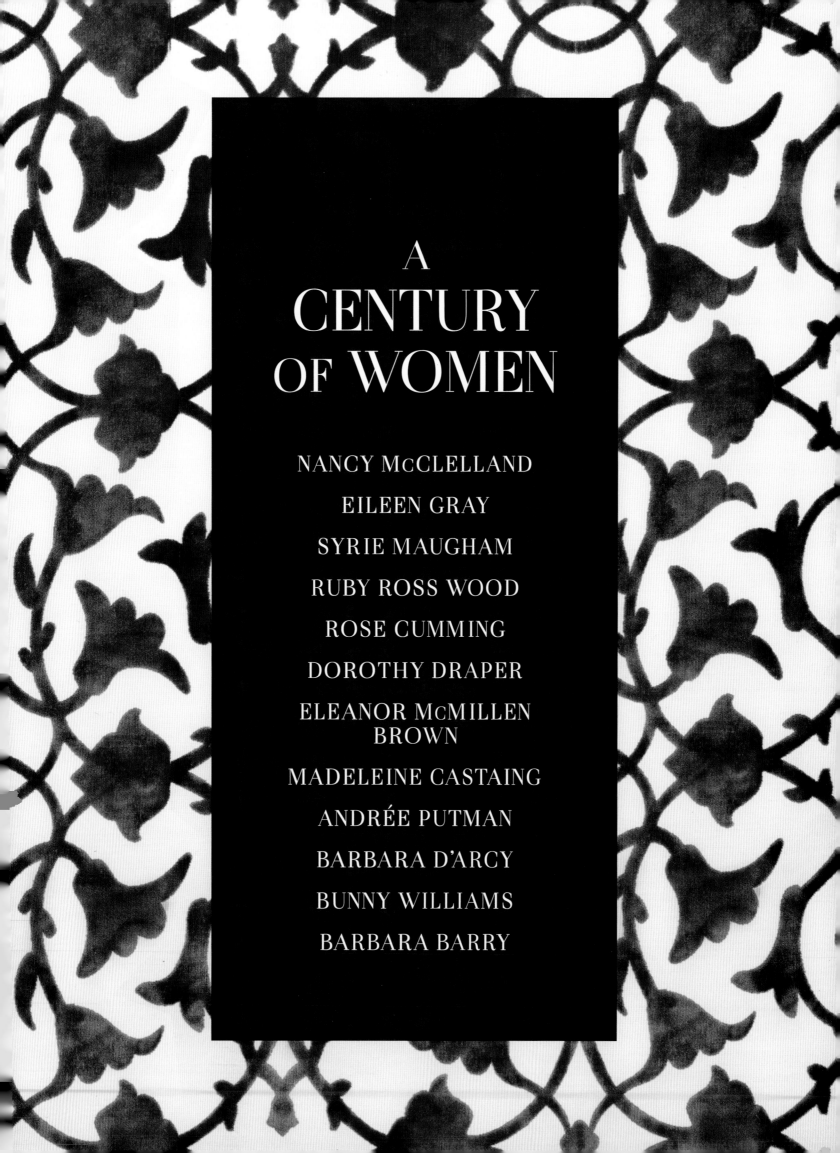

A
CENTURY
OF WOMEN

NANCY McCLELLAND

EILEEN GRAY

SYRIE MAUGHAM

RUBY ROSS WOOD

ROSE CUMMING

DOROTHY DRAPER

ELEANOR McMILLEN
BROWN

MADELEINE CASTAING

ANDRÉE PUTMAN

BARBARA D'ARCY

BUNNY WILLIAMS

BARBARA BARRY

7 | Nancy McClelland
1877–1959

> "I don't know what special qualifications I had for the work except a great delight and love for beautiful old things."

Today's designers may not recognize Nancy McClelland's name, but they owe her a debt of gratitude. A contemporary of Elsie de Wolfe and Ruby Ross Wood, the serious-minded McClelland, one of the design industry's earliest and most ardent advocates, **played a significant role in making interior design a legitimate profession.** "Fed up" that no dictionary provided an adequate definition of a decorator, she helped to organize a nationally publicized effort in the 1930s to formalize the role of the interior designer by devising a standard definition that emphasized education and training.

Vassar-educated, McClelland became renowned for her expertise on antiques and historical wallpapers, subsequently documented in her series of influential books. Her first work, *Historic Wall-Papers*, published in 1924, remains an authoritative resource on the subject. So keen was her interest in antique wallpapers that, in an early example of designer branding, she expanded her decorating business to include a namesake line of reproduction papers. McClelland's role as an industry leader was cemented when she became one of the founding members, and later the first female president, of the American Institute of Interior Decorators, now known as ASID.

But her greatest popular influence was the founding of Au Quatrième, the decorating and antiques division of the long-gone Wanamaker's department store in New York City. A novel idea when introduced in 1913, Au Quatrième was a resounding success, establishing the new "department stores" as influencers of popular taste. A long line of decorators would go on to cut their teeth at retail establishments, including Ruby Ross Wood, who succeeded McClelland at Wanamaker's, William Pahlmann at Lord & Taylor, Barbara D'Arcy at Bloomingdale's, and too many to name at Ralph Lauren. But Nancy McClelland was the first.

Left A desk was an appropriate setting for McClelland, who was one of the best educated, and most academic, of early twentieth-century designers. **Above left** A hallmark of McClelland's work was her use of wallpaper, usually antique. An authority on historical wall-coverings, the decorator launched a collection of reproduction papers. **Opposite** Like many of her fellow lady decorators, McClelland dabbled in high-style modern flourishes, such as these wrought iron trees, accented with melon-shaped lights, on a twenties-era high-rise terrace.

8 | Eileen Gray
1878–1976

"Clients did not come—they found what I did upsetting. This is funny, isn't it?"

Modernism's early practitioners were an old-boy network of architects who took a clinical approach to interior design. The exception was **Eileen Gray, who brought the concept of luxury to their bare-bones world of form and function.**

An Irishwoman, Gray moved to Paris in 1902, where her fine arts studies evolved into one of her earliest successes: lacquered furniture. Using centuries-old Asian techniques, Gray designed pieces of such Art Deco splendor they became the toast of Jazz Age Paris, and well beyond. In 2009, Gray's lacquered Dragons chair sold for $28 million at the auction of the Yves Saint Laurent estate, a record price for early twentieth-century furniture.

But despite the fame it brought her, Gray's lacquer phase was short-lived. In an artistic about-face, she rejected conventional furniture and embraced the Machine Age, adopting an entirely new set of materials: chrome and tubular steel. At first, she applied her newfound viewpoint to furniture design, the best example being the plump leather and steel Bibendum chair, which looks more than a little like the Michelin Man, for whom the chair was named.

Her pioneering vision was fully expressed, however, in what is now considered a crowning achievement of early modernist architecture: E.1027, the minimal yet luxurious house she designed in the late 1920s on the French coast near Nice, at the border with Italy. Gray conceived a home for herself that was practical—with built-in furniture throughout—yet without the sterility of, say, the work of Le Corbusier. He, it seems, was so jealous of the home's success he later vandalized it by painting murals on its white walls. But it is the furniture Gray designed for the house for which she is best remembered, especially her adjustable glass and tubular-steel E1027 drinks table, with its distinctive chain—one of the most enduring examples of early-modernist furniture still in production today.

Above left Photographed in her adopted city of Paris in 1926, the stylish Gray cut quite a figure among the city's smartest circles.
Left Gray's 1923 Monte Carlo Room, a bedroom-boudoir conceived for an exhibition, allowed the designer to display her skill with luxurious finishes, including a black-lacquered divan with fur cover, a dark-red-and-white lacquered screen, and a ceiling light made of parchment.

Right In E.1027, her innovative home near Nice, Gray revolutionized the International style with her Bibendum chair (left) and Transat chair (right), her interpretation of a deck chair. **Below** Gray's enduring E1027 table, placed bedside in the home's guest room. Gray used strong color, unlike her fellow modernists.

9 | Syrie Maugham
1879–1955

"Elimination is one of the secrets of successful interior design."

Above Around 1930, the photographer Cecil Beaton, an admirer of Maugham, captured the designer as the White Queen, posing her in his trademark fashion: against a stylized backdrop.
Opposite The most celebrated room of 1930s London, Maugham's music room, in her King's Road home, was a carefully orchestrated ensemble of whites and creams, a mirrored screen, a low table by Jean-Michel Frank, and a modern rug by Marion Dorn.
Overleaf Glamour defined Maugham's work, especially her Mayfair bedroom for Rebecca Sieff in 1936. Amid the draped satin and sheepskin rug was an upholstered sleigh bed, a Maugham signature.

Syrie Maugham was an English maverick who defined the look of 1930s glamour. She herself was captivating, prompting Cecil Beaton to call her "a woman with flair and a strong personal taste of her own." The ex-wife of the English writer Somerset Maugham, she was a noted London hostess and friend to the Bright Young Things, including the flamboyant Stephen Tennant, whose house, Wilsford Manor, she helped to decorate with ample yardage of satin and more than a trace of baroque pastiche.

Maugham frequently bent the rules, especially when it came to antique furniture, which she often had pickled or stripped bare of its finish. It's hard to imagine anything that could have been more shocking in England at the time. Then there was her penchant for plaster palm-tree columns and furniture, which lent a previously unimaginable theatricality to many upper-class English homes.

But it was the color white that earned the designer transatlantic fame as well as the sobriquet, the White Queen. Assisted by her pickling and plaster, Maugham spawned a craze for whitewashed rooms that, along with portraits by Cecil Beaton and Constance Spry floral arrangements, spelled chic to Londoners between the wars. To be fair, other designers, such as Elsie de Wolfe, were experimenting with white, too, but it was Maugham who provided the decade-defining example of it: her own all-white music room, described in *Vogue* as: "Bare white plaster walls, furniture done up in whitewash satin and brocade, silver curtains, a white rug by Marion Dorn, flaring white peacock feathers."

Within just a few years of their unveiling, white rooms would seem passé. Maugham changed direction with the fashion, and showed equal command of vibrant colors: her scheme for the vivid Chinese-papered Palm Beach living room of Mona and Harrison Williams, immortalized in a famous Beaton illustration, is just one example. Nevertheless, her association with the color white has stuck, and it is that for which she will always be remembered.

10 | Ruby Ross Wood
1880–1950

"It's when they stop copying you that it's time to worry."

Despite her sideways start in the interior design world—as a young journalist, she ghostwrote Elsie de Wolfe's *The House in Good Taste*—Ruby Ross Wood eventually joined the ranks of the great lady decorators, gaining attention in part because of her trademark rose-colored glasses. Unyielding about herself—she notoriously wore sweaters and coats to keep warm in the summer and was known to play solitaire for hours in lieu of physical exercise—Wood was deceptively adventurous when it came to decorating, fearlessly mixing previously unmixable furnishings to create rooms unlike those of any other designer.

For example, there was the Manhattan dining room she conceived for the young Brooke Astor. On the one hand, the room dazzled with thirties-era glamour thanks to sleek white walls and a gleaming glass fireplace mantel, on which a pair of avant-garde Jean-Michel Frank plaster masks were displayed. And yet demurely holding court in the center of the room were a very traditional Directoire fruitwood table and chairs. It was a surprising combination, but like all her

dashing efforts, it worked. Equally unexpected were Wood's daring color combinations, like the brown, black, and white scheme she chose for another client's dining room. It might be hard to fathom today, but this color medley was considered radical in the early 1930s.

Her own talent aside, Wood can claim credit for one of the century's greatest decorators, Billy Baldwin. She took the young Baldwin under her wing when he moved to New York City and honed his style until, like his mentor, he was always two steps ahead of everyone else. As Baldwin once wrote of her, "She was quite simply the finest decorator who ever lived."

Above According to Billy Baldwin, Ruby Ross Wood wore a "usual costume: veiled hat, clanking gold bracelet, round rose-colored glasses." **Opposite** A mirrored fireplace, jauntily trimmed slipper chairs, and white carpet, in the H. Mercer Walkers' Manhattan apartment in 1937, are classic Wood flair. **Overleaf** Wood decorated this remarkably timeless living room for the Wolcott Blairs in a buffed-out palette. The "slipcovered" desk is pure Wood.

11 | Rose Cumming
1887–1968

"Muted tones ... are my enemies."

Marked by aesthetic madness and a faded Sunset Boulevard aura, Rose Cumming, the Australian expat who moved to Manhattan in 1917 and took up decorating out of boredom, was one of the design world's most original originals. At times, her work could be the very picture of propriety: ladylike antiques, damask upholstery, English paneling, and floral-strewn fabrics. But more often than not, puddled curtains aside, Cumming's style was far more curious than anything ever seen on Manhattan's Upper East Side. Starting with her violet-tinted hair ...

To those who knew her—including the designers Mario Buatta, Mark Hampton, and Tom Britt, who all, as young men, willingly spent the occasional Saturday cleaning her glamorous West Fifty-Third Street townhouse— **Cumming was weird and wonderful, and the same thing could be said of her work.** Her color combinations (think blues paired with purples) were off-beat but ravishing, as were the densely patterned, strangely colored fabrics bearing banana leaves, leopard spots (in pink, no less), and lush delphiniums that were sold through her much-vaunted Madison Avenue antiques shop. Then there was her fondness for Coromandel screens, antique Chinese wallpaper, Foo dogs, and pagodas, which suffused her work with the atmosphere of the Celestial Empire. Mirror, crystal, silver leaf, and even lamé—drama lurked around every corner.

In her legendary townhouse, Cumming became infamous for her so-called Ugly Room, a subversive phantasmagoria of beasts, snakes, and all manner of bizarre furnishings. It was macabre and quite unlike her other work, but it was right on-message, establishing her as the designer from whom one should expect the unexpected.

Opposite Cumming, photographed for an issue of *Harper's Bazaar* wearing a Turkish robe in her legendary Manhattan fabrics and antiques shop. **Below** A reflection of Cumming's proudly eccentric personality, the so-called Ugly Room in her West Fifty-Third Street townhouse was notable for its "sinister, ugly, destructive, or macabre objects and decorations."

More typical of Cumming's feminine style was her drawing room, with its eighteenth-century Chinese wallpaper. "It was really a drawing room," a dazzled Tom Britt recalled. Despite its beauty, it lacked "lounging furniture."

12 | Dorothy Draper
1889–1969

"Don't ever be afraid to experiment with old things—some of the smartest effects were achieved because someone used brains instead of money!"

A bustling design practice, a series of books, hotel projects, licensed product collections, advertising endorsements—common aspirations for today's ambitious designers, but for Dorothy Draper, an early twentieth-century trailblazer in designer branding, all were breakthroughs in an innovative career. Born in the upper-crust enclave of Tuxedo Park, New York, Draper overcame the social confines of her class and her lack of formal training, boldly launching a decorating business in 1920s Manhattan. A savvy marketer—perhaps one of the best this business has ever known—she managed to parlay a few early residential projects into a string of high-profile commercial jobs, including the interiors of the Carlyle Hotel and Hampshire House in New York, and the Mark Hopkins Hotel in San Francisco.

The Draper look was bold, particularly in the hotels she decorated. Black-and-white checkerboard floors, baroque plaster ornamentation, jewel-colored walls paired with wide-striped fabrics and cabbage-rose chintzes, and overscaled everything—no lampshade ever seemed big enough for her—all defined Draper's work. Nowhere was this more evident than in her dazzling decorative scheme for the Greenbrier resort in West Virginia, the masterpiece of her career.

Her much-publicized design projects brought her acclaim. But it was her series of how-to books (most notably her 1939 bible *Decorating is Fun!*, which blithely encouraged readers to bleach their Oriental rugs and take a saw to the legs of antique tables); her mass-market collections of fabrics, furniture, and even gift wrap; and her nationally syndicated newspaper column that made her a household name. **With the marketing skills to match all that talent, Draper created the blueprint from which scores of designers have since built their careers.**

Above Draper, seen here in 1942, was the most publicized, and perhaps most photographed, decorator of her day.
Opposite Oversize lacquered lampshades and beefy stripes, preferably five inches wide, were constants throughout Draper's work.

Above Checkerboard floors and baroque plaster flourishes—unmistakable Draper style—greeted guests at the Camellia House restaurant in Chicago's Drake Hotel. **Opposite** Draper's flair for the theatrical was evident at the Greenbrier resort, where a wall clock was dramtized with showy plasterwork.

Overleaf At the Metropolitan Museum of Art in New York, the designer outfitted a now-lost restaurant, nicknamed the Dorotheum, with birdcage chandeliers, black-and-white columns, and nymphs frolicking in a pool.

13 | Eleanor McMillen Brown

1890–1991

"There is nothing more trite than a set period."

Top A McMillen Inc. room always projected propriety, as did Eleanor McMillen Brown herself. **Above** No slave to convention, Brown could also be daring, as when she decorated this St. Louis living room in the late 1930s using an unusual eggplant-colored fabric on the walls. **Opposite** Brown became a favorite designer of the American upper class, including Mrs. Henry Ford II, whose bedroom is illustrated here. **Overleaf** Brown first decorated her Sutton Place apartment in 1928, including this cheery yellow living room. Over the decades, until her death, she rarely changed a thing.

Always respectfully addressed as Mrs. Brown by her employees and peers alike, Eleanor McMillen Brown, who played a role at her firm until her nineties, had what might well have been the lengthiest career of any interior designer.

No doubt influenced by her rich entrepreneurial father, who was a cofounder of Magic Chef stoves, Brown brought a businesslike approach to decorating, and **arguably turned the ad hoc women's world she entered into a profession with standards.** After taking secretarial classes and studying at the Parsons School of Design, she worked briefly for the esteemed designer Elsie Cobb Wilson, and in 1924 founded her own firm, naming it McMillen Inc. She even insisted that all her employees be Parsons graduates, too. "I thought if I was going to do it at all, I'd better do it professionally," she said. "That's why it's McMillen Inc. and not Eleanor McMillen. I wasn't one of the 'ladies.'"

As poised and polished as her work, Brown quickly found success decorating for her upper-class friends, for whom she devised posh rooms that, in turn, made McMillen Inc. a synonym for impeccable taste and correctness. A well-heeled mix of mostly eighteenth-century French antiques and modern furnishings became a McMillen signature, as did mild-mannered color palettes. A sign of good breeding for a certain circle, the McMillen style even made its way into the newlywed home of Sister Parish, whose mother enlisted Brown's expertise as a wedding gift. Parish later crabbed, "I never forgave my mother."

The financially savvy Brown so successfully laid McMillen's foundation that it remains one of Manhattan's premier design firms. A tour through McMillen polished the résumés of a generation of celebrated interior designers, including Albert Hadley and Mark Hampton. But one of Brown's more interesting achievements was the fierce loyalty she earned from her employees. Many talented designers worked under the McMillen flag for the duration of their careers, notably Betty Sherrill, whose nearly forty-year tenure at McMillen made her a legend, like Mrs. Brown.

14 | Madeleine Castaing
1894–1992

> "Personally, I just follow my instinct, amuse myself creating an atmosphere, mix up all sorts of things I like."

The Proust of twentieth-century decorating, Madeleine Castaing held court for decades in her antiques shop on the rue Jacob in Paris, welcoming admirers and refusing to sell much of anything to anybody. She possessed an independent streak that made both her and her work anachronisms in their time, and even today, her work maintains an air of mystery. While the majority of her peers were experimenting with the latest fashions, Castaing defiantly immersed her work squarely in the nineteenth century.

Difficult to pigeon-hole, her interiors paid homage to no one particular historical style, instead representing a patchwork of often unfashionable influences. English Regency and Napoleon III furniture were particular favorites of hers, as was leopard-print carpet, an Empire-period fashion. Her rooms were filled with black accents; she especially loved ebonized furniture. A certain shade of blue, somewhere in the neighborhood of a

Tiffany box, will forever belong to her and her alone. A sense of decay pervaded her rooms, whether achieved intentionally, through the use of furnishings "past their prime," or by mistake, in the tears and stains that the designer preferred not to mend. Castaing would channel the romantic past and conceal a room's origins until it seemed formed over a great length of time, in stark contrast to the pristine—and, in her mind, soulless— work of her contemporaries.

Given that she lived through some of the most dazzling moments in twentieth-century modernism—Paris in the twenties comes to mind—the fact that her work makes not even the slightest reference to them is remarkable and even radical. Deeply nostalgic and sentimental to her core, Castaing was a voice in the wilderness, not least for her unforgettable appearance: extravagant false lashes, overly made-up red lips, and a bob-length wig conspicuously held in place by a chin strap.

Opposite Part of Castaing's persona was her extraordinary appearance, including her wig's visible chin strap and her overly made-up lips and eyes. **Left** The Grand Salon of Castaing's apartment in Paris. "New" and "sparkling" were not in the designer's vocabulary. Downstairs was her fabled shop.

At Lèves, Castaing's cherished country house near Chartres, the designer's romantic style was on full display in her trademark leopard-print carpet and "Castaing blue" coolie lampshades.

15 | Andrée Putman

1925–2013

> "If you give in to all the temptations of adding, you introduce the drop of poison that will age what you've done."

The 1980s were a series of wildly different design trends, from the quaint—the simple pleasures of country living providing a respite from the decade's grandiosity—to the quirky, culminating in the oddball furniture of the Memphis Group. But cutting like a knife through the tangle of competing tastes was *le style Putman*, the sleek and sometimes severe look of French designer Andrée Putman. A self-labeled "archaeologist of modernity," Putman sought inspiration from early modernism, dramatizing its rigor into a style all her own.

As sharp as the padded-shouldered silhouette made famous by those other eighties-defining French powerhouses, the fashion designers Thierry Mugler and Claude Montana, Putman's work was precise, disciplined, and

rarely prone to embellishment. "Sweet and clean envelopes for exceptional human beings" was how she once described her interiors, which were admired by an exceptional clientele that included Karl Lagerfeld, Azzedine Alaïa, and Yves Saint Laurent. Barring her signature crimson lipstick, Putman dressed the way she decorated, in a monochromatic palette of white, black, and—sometimes—gray. Patterned fabrics were not even a possibility. Said the designer, "prints are an aggression you never asked for." Models of restraint, Putman's rooms were striking for what little was in them: reproductions of twenties- and thirties-era modernist furniture by Eileen Gray, Jean-Michel Frank, and Pierre Chareau, whose designs Putman licensed and made popular again through her company Ecart International.

A celebrity in her native France, Putman finally conquered America in the middle of the eighties, when she was hired by Studio 54 impresarios Ian Schrager and Steve Rubell to remake the old Morgans Hotel in Manhattan, which she did in groundbreaking fashion. A statement-making black-and-white lobby reminiscent of a disco, minimally appointed guest rooms devoid of color, black-and-white-checkerboard tiled bathrooms, and Robert Mapplethorpe photography all established the hotel as the temple of cutting-edge chic. An instant success when it opened in 1984, Morgans launched the boutique-hotel craze that has yet to wane decades later. Looking back, **Putman's work was the template for the mass marketing of hipness.**

Opposite Putman practiced what she preached, wearing a monochromatic wardrobe as tightly edited as her interiors.
Left Some of the most talked-about bathrooms of the late twentieth century were in Morgans Hotel in Manhattan, where Putman's use of black-and-white checkerboard tile caused a sensation.

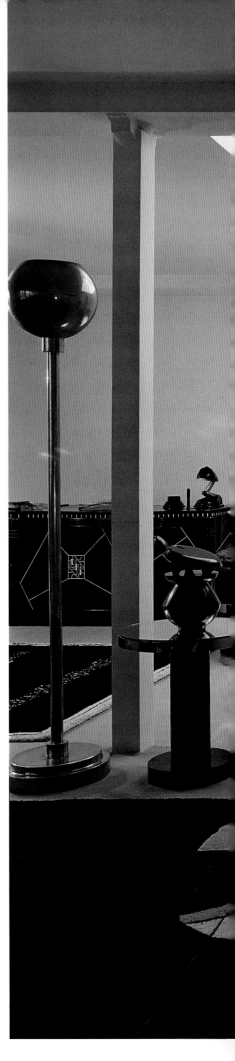

Above French Minister of Culture Jack Lang's Paris office, designed by Putman in 1984, underscored the designer's belief in "sumptuous austerity." **Right** "Light and space are the stars," Putman said, and nowhere was this more true than in her own loft in Paris, one of the city's most exciting and influential interiors in the 1980s.

16 | Barbara D'Arcy
1928–2012

"In those sixteen years [at Bloomingdale's], I got out of my system everything I could ever think of."

Top Although she explored every style under the sun, Barbara D'Arcy proved most creative when working with cutting-edge materials. Above The Bloomingdale's model room that caused the biggest splash was the Cave Room, with undulating walls made of sprayed foam. Opposite For another model, D'Arcy fashioned an acrylic platform and colored lights into a bedroom that spelled the future.

The year is 1973. You're a New Yorker. It's Sunday, and after quiche and Bloody Marys with your friends at brunch, you slip on your yellow-tinted aviators and head where all sophisticated New Yorkers head—for a stroll through the crush at the most unique singles bar in New York: the model rooms at Bloomingdale's department store.

Zen. Scandinavian. Tuscan. Provençal. The Egypt of King Tut. Modern and ... inflatable. Who else but Barbara D'Arcy, the designer responsible for these legendary rooms, can claim credit for decorating spaces of such staggering variety? She had complete freedom to let her imagination run wild, and was quite possibly the only decorator ever not to be burdened with pesky clients. D'Arcy spent the 1960s and 1970s executing vignettes so sensational they attracted not only shoppers, but became required viewing for fellow designers, the media, and style setters in every field.

Whether they were flights of fancy, as D'Arcy called her zanier efforts, or more traditionally appointed, the designer decorated every room with the kind of attention not usually lavished on department store settings. Built around themes, each room was an environment, with fully fleshed out decorative schemes against very believable architecture and scenic backdrops. Her Cave Room, for example, was a futuristic grotto with a mirrored floor and an illuminated Plexiglas dining table surrounded by undulating white walls made of sprayed foam. Yet she was equally capable of doing a historical re-creation of an Elizabethan manor house down to its rough-hewn timber and beams.

In those years, Bloomingdale's was always one step ahead of everybody, and D'Arcy was the disseminator of nonstop trends and new furniture styles; it was she who helped introduce architect Frank Gehry's cardboard furniture to the general public. She might have been motivated by selling merchandise, but her influence on American taste was far more consequential than just that. **With a stage that gave her a reach far greater than any other designer, D'Arcy was a major player in shaping the look of the late twentieth-century American home.**

17 | Bunny Williams
1944–

"Even more important than the food is the atmosphere you create—that's what people are really going to remember."

Above Assuming the role once occupied by Sister Parish, Bunny Williams is today's grande dame of American decorating. **Opposite** "I can't imagine not having a beautiful bedroom," says Williams, whose own New York City bedroom is built around a mirrored four-poster. **Overleaf** This well-proportioned living room in Virginia gave Williams the space to do what she does best: make a room balanced and functional through masterfully placed furniture.

The most high-profile alumna of Parish-Hadley Associates, Bunny Williams followed the best education a designer could receive with a huge career. A respected traditionalist in the vein of Sister Parish, Williams knows instinctively how to make a house functional and beautiful. Yet unlike Parish, Williams is precise and methodical when planning a room, a discipline encouraged by the meticulous Albert Hadley. "Albert made me the designer I am. She [Parish] made me the decorator I am."

Famous for creating some of the most livable interiors around—"when a room is lived in, you can feel it," she once wrote—Williams lavishes rooms with the attention they need to work. **Her beautifully balanced furniture plans, an art dying fast in the era of the sectional, are masterful.** Seating is indulgent and convenient to drinks tables—a boon for any guest in it for the long haul. Lighting flatters both the room and its occupants. If it seems as if Williams designs her rooms with entertaining in mind, it's because she herself is a well-known hostess, who is always prepared for spur-of-the-moment gatherings by stocking her freezer with cheese straws and miniature sausage biscuits, both delicacies reflective of her Southern upbringing.

But as carefully chosen as everything is, Williams makes sure to do what many designers are loath to do: give a room the impression of her never having been there. A master of the undecorated look, Williams layers rooms with textiles, antique furniture, and one-off accessories, all of which appear to have been gathered over time, not necessarily culled in one sweep.

Williams concurrently heads a thriving design practice based in New York; has written several books, including one of the most successful design books ever published, *An Affair With a House*; lectures at scores of events; and oversees a network of licensed product lines that have made her one of today's most successful American designers. And with her husband, the furniture and antiques dealer John Rosselli, there may be no greater design power couple in New York.

18 | Barbara Barry
1952–

"Design is a religion to me."

Like Elsie de Wolfe before her, California designer Barbara Barry considers interior design a spiritual calling and has made it her life's mission "to help people live a beautiful life."

Her work is the picture of self-composure, with nary a hair out of place. She swept away the chintzes and fringes of the 1980s and ushered in the modern era of dark woods silhouetted against creamy walls. When there was color, it was limited to the pale and pastel—peach, celadon—forming a palette distinctly her own. Patternless, her rooms were blemish-free. And they had the unmistakable Art Deco glamour of her home city, Los Angeles, though reminiscent more of the cool blonde than the platinum siren.

Still, Barry would say her mission goes deeper, intended to enhance all aspects of living, even the most mundane. "It's the small things we see and touch every day that leave an impression and give us serenity." For her, those small things include drinking tea only from a porcelain cup and decanting detergent into an attractive vessel, a practice that will likely forever be associated with the designer.

Through it all, the woman has styled herself to look astonishingly like her rooms, cultivating an immaculate appearance that almost always includes kitten heels, pearl necklaces, and swing skirts, not to mention her much-envied coif, which is perfectly tousled. Graduating from the role of interior designer to that of lifestyle designer, **Barry became one of the 1990s' most bankable brands**, one that continues to thrive today. With books, furniture, bed linens, china, and even a line of teas to her name, Barry designs her product collections as she does her interiors: with a clear sense of purpose. "It's not about how much we have but about how what we have serves us."

***

Above left Partial to soft colors and quiet fabrics, Barbara Barry is "not a chintz gal." **Left** Known for rooms with clean lines, Barry likens design to tea: "What you leave out is as important as what you put in." **Opposite** Some suggestion of Art Deco and Hollywood glamour always comes through in Barry's work.

1929

THE
INFLUENCERS

VANESSA BELL

HENRY FRANCIS
DU PONT

CEDRIC GIBBONS

CHARLES
DE BEISTEGUI

CECIL BEATON

PAULINE POTTER
DE ROTHSCHILD

RODERICK CAMERON

19 | Vanessa Bell
1879–1961

A key figure in the Bloomsbury Group, the influential—if emotionally tangled—artistic and literary circle that included the early twentieth-century English writers Virginia Woolf and Lytton Strachey, Vanessa Bell (Woolf's sister) was a painter of some regard. But it was her contributions to the decorative arts—in particular, her free-spirited approach to design at a time when it was stodgy and codified—for which she earned more lasting fame. **She defines the stylish bohemian to this day.**

One of Bell's early forays into decoration was as a director of the celebrated Omega Workshops, founded in 1913 by another of the Bloomsbury set, Roger Fry, as an experiment marrying the fine and applied arts. A collective of artists, the studio created an array of household items, including fabrics, ceramics, and furniture, which were embellished with colorful, painterly, and often naive abstract designs—original stuff for a society still in the throes of Edwardian propriety.

Bell's style flourished at Charleston, the Sussex farmhouse she shared with her children; her husband; her lover, Duncan Grant; and Grant's male lover, who would later marry Bell's daughter by Grant. As the writer Dorothy Parker said, "they lived in squares, painted in circles, and loved in triangles." Their lives were complicated to be sure, but Charleston's interiors were, in contrast, lively and carefree, embellished with Bell and Grant's artistry. Walls, mantels, moldings, lampshades, and even fabrics were painted with colorful figures and patterns, which, depending on your point of view, made Charleston one of the most beguiling, or one of the scruffiest-looking, houses in England. Now open to the public as a museum, Charleston continues to earn an almost cultlike admiration among today's design mavericks.

Above left Bell, photographed in 1907, a decade before her decorative efforts began at Charleston. **Left** Bell's masterpiece was Charleston, in the Downs of England, where she embellished walls, trim, and even this dining table with her hand-painted designs. **Opposite** Bell and her lover, the artist Duncan Grant, conceived this music room for London's Lefèvre Gallery in the early 1930s. The couple's fondness for hand-drawn embellishments is on full display here.

20 | Henry Francis du Pont
1880–1969

> "I had always thought of American furniture as just kitchen furniture. I didn't dream it had so much richness and variety."

American furniture and crafts were considered inferior to English antiques before Henry Francis du Pont, the chemical-company heir, used his family fortune to amass a superb, and prolific, collection of Americana over a lifetime. It was so beautifully displayed at his family's estate, Winterthur, outside Wilmington, Delaware, that his house would one day become one of this country's most prestigious museums.

With a passion for the domestic arts, du Pont decorated Winterthur in period fashion—each room assigned an American historical style—but in a stylish, luxurious manner, earning him admiration from Jacqueline Kennedy, Sister Parish, and even Diana Vreeland. An inveterate host, du Pont would receive his guests in the Port Royal Parlor,

with its Philadelphia Chippendale–style furniture, before later enjoying cocktails and cards in the Chinese Parlor, so named for its 1770s hand-painted Chinese wallpaper. So diligent was du Pont in his pursuit of authenticity that the house was illuminated at night by candlelight, save for the gooseneck lamps brought as a concession to each guest's bedroom. Recalling the comforts he experienced during a weekend visit to Winterthur, Billy Baldwin wrote, "nothing old-fashioned here but the charm."

Opened to the public as a museum in 1951, **Winterthur not only established du Pont as an authority on Americana, it also elevated the status of the American decorative arts, earning them a rightful place in the larger world of antiques.**

Opposite "Early American Arts and Crafts had not been given the recognition they deserved," prompting Henry Francis du Pont to turn Winterthur into this country's leading decorative arts museum.
Left The Port Royal Parlor, with its eighteenth-century paneling and Philadelphia Chippendale–style furniture, is one of Winterthur's most significant rooms.

21 | Cedric Gibbons

1893–1960

Since the early days of the twentieth century, movies and interior design have had a close relationship, with each influencing the other. **The man who forged the link between the two by creating movie sets so drop-dead glamorous that filmgoers wanted to live in them** was Cedric Gibbons, the legendary Metro-Goldwyn-Mayer art director who designed the look of some of Hollywood's most memorable movies—and even the Oscar statuette.

It was Gibbons who brought Art Deco to the movies, making it synonymous with sophisticated living for the American public. Introduced to the daring style at the legendary 1925 Exposition Internationale des Arts Décoratifs et Industriels Modernes, the Paris design exhibition from which the style takes its name, Gibbons imported what he saw to Hollywood and adapted its Jazz Age energy for the wildly successful 1928 silent film *Our Dancing Daughters*. The modernistic sets—think Art Deco setbacks and ziggurat motifs—captured the public's imagination and emboldened many moviegoers to experiment with modern decoration in their own homes. (The movie, which dramatized the perils of Roaring Twenties flappers' wanton ways, also helped catapult Joan Crawford to stardom.) Gibbons would go on to oversee the sets of countless movies from the golden age of Hollywood: *Grand Hotel, The Thin Man, The Wizard of Oz,* and *The Philadelphia Story*. His work was so influential he is credited with introducing Venetian blinds and indirect lighting to American houses.

Though not a residential designer, Gibbons was responsible for one of the great examples of early modernism in Los Angeles: a dramatic Streamline Moderne house, built in the early 1930s, for him and his wife, actress Dolores del Río, whose beauty was said to have inspired Gibbons's lavish use of mirror throughout the interior. A dazzling film set come to life, the house—recently restored and decorated by the very talented interior designer Madeline Stuart, and as revered as ever—is Gibbons's legacy as much as any of his films.

Opposite Cedric Gibbons, with his wife, the actress Dolores del Río, in their living room. Beginning in the 1920s, he influenced American ideas about decorating and glamour with his revolutionary, highly stylized film sets—the "white telephone look." **Below** The Los Angeles house that Gibbons designed for himself and del Río in the early 1930s is one the most important remaining examples of the Streamline Moderne style.

22 | Charles de Beistegui
1895–1970

> "I feel strongly that true creativity can only take place when the past is brought into play."

Above Of the aesthete and collector Charles de Beistegui, Cecil Beaton wrote, "His imagination is so rich that his imitators can never keep up with him or guess what he will make fashionable tomorrow." **Opposite** Beistegui's many collections were displayed densely and dramatically in the library at his celebrated Château de Groussay.

Not the most likeable member of café society—"utterly ruthless" was how one acquaintance described him—Charles de Beistegui, a French-born scion blessed with a Mexican silver mining fortune, was miserly, snobbish, and a womanizer who, it has been said, paid little heed to those below the rank of duchess. But when it came to his taste, there was much to admire. Beistegui so artfully arranged his houses that his decorating prowess was sought out by fellow socialites, despite the fact that he was not a professional. Baron de Redé, one such recipient of Beistegui's expertise, remarked, "If he had not been so rich, he would have made a fabulous interior decorator."

Beistegui's first great design adventure played out in his Paris apartment, which he made over in the 1930s with the help of friend and frequent collaborator, the Cuban-born architect Emilio Terry. Fool-the-eye quilted walls, mirrored draperies, and a rooftop terrace resembling an outdoor formal living room all reflected the thirties-era vogue for Surrealism. **Avant-garde in every way, Beistegui's efforts set a new fashion for decorative fantasy.**

For his next project, his French country estate, Château de Groussay, the tastemaker had to get ahead of the fashion once again. Representing not one style but, instead, a melting pot, Groussay was at heart an English country house, but with Continental flair nobody had ever quite seen. A two-story library capturing the moodiness of the late nineteenth century and a Dutch-style salon finished with blue-and-white Delft tile were just two of the rooms that earned Groussay its reputation as a pleasure dome of design originality. But for all of Beistegui's money, the quality of his home's furnishings was spotty at best; as long as something visually pleased him, he was satisfied.

Groussay elevated decorating to an art form and was considered hallowed ground by generations of designers, including Mario Buatta, Miles Redd, and David Hicks, who was uncharacteristically generous in crediting Beistegui's style as an influence. In the words of one French aristocrat, "Everything Beistegui created or imagined became a model for the decorators of our time."

Before he mingled French and English historical styles at Groussay, Beistegui experimented with modernism in his Paris apartment, adding baroque-style furniture to Le Corbusier's architecture.

23 | Cecil Beaton
1904–1980

> "I have the reputation of being sensational and staggering."

Opposite Cecil Beaton in repose in his deep-red, flocked-wallpaper drawing room at Reddish House, 1950. **Above** One of Beaton's most audacious efforts was his Circus Bedroom at Ashcombe. Beaton friends Rex Whistler and Oliver Messel contributed to the room's murals. **Overleaf** The Reddish drawing room photographed thirty years later. Beaton once recounted the many decorative styles he had explored, including "the baroque, the surrealist, the neo-Gothic. I've been through all the Louis's, most of the Georges, at least one Edward and all of Victoria."

His highly stylized photographic portraits helped set the dazzling tone for the 1930s, while decades later, his sets and costume designs for the 1964 film *My Fair Lady* won two Oscars. A writer and an inexhaustible social gadfly, Cecil Beaton spent his adulthood relentlessly courting VIPs, very likely in reaction to his insecurity about being born middle class. Socialites and artists were his early targets, while later conquests included café society and the ultimate quarry: the royal family. Among those he pursued most ardently was actress Greta Garbo, with whom Beaton conducted an obsessive romantic relationship that still ranks as one of the last century's stranger couplings. **Best remembered for his published diaries whose name-dropping entries remain required reading, Beaton relished playing the role of aesthete, using his flair for the dramatic in several landmark houses to advance his ambitions.**

It was at Ashcombe House, Beaton's much-loved country retreat (later owned by Madonna), where he allowed his creativity to run riot, fashioning rooms of such theatricality they had the appearance of being stages, which in a way they were. There was his Circus Bedroom, so named for its merry-go-round bed and big-top murals, and a bathroom whose walls were painted with the outlines of his prominent guests' hands—a country house guest book of sorts. A lesson in exuberance gone slightly mad, the interior of Ashcombe flew in the face of conventionality and likely endeared Beaton (up the social ladder) to his fellow rule-breakers, the Bright Young Things. Beaton was so enamored of Ashcombe that when his landlord refused to extend his lease on the house, he said he felt as if "galloping cancer had been diagnosed."

Although Beaton's later homes in London and the country, notably Reddish House, reflected an aesthetic maturity that relied less on gimmicks, they never lapsed into stylistic complacency. Always flirting with fashion and never quite correct in the Colefax & Fowler way—Reddish was once described as "the epitome of delicately perfumed Edwardiana"—Beaton's dandyish homes beckoned a younger generation of tastemakers, including Nicky Haslam. A frequent visitor to Beaton's London house, Haslam fell under its spell, eventually renting it after Beaton's death and keeping its "astonishing" Beaton-era decor intact.

24 | Pauline Potter de Rothschild

1908–1976

"It is now empty, which as you know is what I consider true comfort."

Opposite "Everything Pauline de Rothschild touches turns to loveliness," according to perhaps her greatest admirer, Billy Baldwin. **Above** In Rothschild's London bedroom, a portrait painting dominated the room, while a chaise bed rounded out the spartan, but elegant, setting.

A traumatic childhood in Paris and a Baltimore debut gave little indication of what young Pauline Potter would eventually become: a tastemaker of such ineffable style that she sent people into fits of rapture. To Billy Baldwin, a close friend who exhaustively credited her with influencing his own style, she was, simply put, "one of the world's finest specimens of civilized humanity."

It was in the 1940s, as a young fashion designer living in New York City, that she began to formulate *le style Pauline*, which she cultivated as assiduously as her persona. There, in an early apartment, she cannily placed a humble wicker basket of flowers on top of an elegant French commode, a high-low gesture unheard of at the time, which later informed a particular brand of American sophistication that was embraced by Baldwin himself and later, the socialite Bunny Mellon. But it was in France, as chatelaine of Mouton, the château she shared with her husband, Baron Philippe de Rothschild, where the style setter was given the means to fully implement her vision. Like all her homes, a curious mix of richness and asceticism, Mouton was rigorously edited and even sparse, but what was present was of exceptional quality. The phrase "second-rate" never entered her vocabulary.

Even the strong-willed John Fowler fell under Rothschild's spell, agreeing to help her furnish her set at London's Albany not in classic English fashion, but rather, as an ethereal-looking evocation of Tsarist Russia. Rothschild would spend the final days of her strange life in this apartment, sleeping upright in a chaise longue in a room bare except for a large painting and elaborate ball-gown curtains only Fowler could have concocted.

Above Rothschild's great gift was the unconventional use of conventional things; in her Paris apartment, tables were unusually low to the ground. Opposite The elaborate curtains in Rothschild's London drawing room, in her set at the Albany, are the only hint that John Fowler was involved in the room's decoration, which was unlike his other work.

25 | Roderick Cameron
1913–1985

"I just can't see myself being nice and charming
to people whose taste I can't fathom."

Opposite Cameron was fascinated by his own abilities, saying,
"I am often surprised at how I know things by instinct." **Above** Later
in life, tastemaker Cameron retreated to his house in Provence;
its sculptural stair hall hinted at the discipline he was known for.
Overleaf Cameron's first great design accomplishment was
La Fiorentina, the French Riviera villa that Mark Hampton said
"was considered by everyone who saw it to be about the chicest
house in the world." (To see Billy Baldwin's version of the house,
turn to page 11.)

Even the most discerning tastemakers must have someone to look up to, and for Van Day Truex and many others who shaped the modern decorating world, that person
was Roderick "Rory" Cameron, the man with the gimlet eye.
A dilettante decorator and author born to privilege—his
mother, Lady Kenmare, was widowed so often it prompted
writer Somerset Maugham to call her Lady Killmore—
Cameron had three distinct advantages according to
admirer Billy Baldwin: "enormous taste, great enthusiasm,
and plenty of money."

With the confidence bestowed by a sizeable fortune,
Cameron had no need to be showy. Instead, **he expressed
his superior taste through a series of houses
whose interiors were so understated, and yet, so
chic, they became symbols of sophistication,
much like a Balenciaga gown.** At La Fiorentina, his
villa on the French Riviera, and many later houses, Cameron
made clear his feelings about color, which Baldwin found so
lacking, he once described La Fiorentina as "a photograph
in black-and- white." Also distinctly missing from his coterie of homes was pattern. Successful where most have failed,
Cameron weaponized subtlety, achieving arresting effects
in spite of the fact that his motives were barely discernible.

Cameron did not hold back, however, when it came to
his likes and dislikes, and when he mentioned them in the
occasional magazine article, admirers took note. Lacquer,
Egyptian and Chinese artifacts, and needlework rugs were
anointed by the holy one. Dark woods, bars and drinks
cabinets ("a horror"), wall-to-wall carpeting, and floral bou-
quets were scorned.

But Cameron reserved special attention for his displays
of objects, which were considered by some to be more
masterful even than those of David Hicks. As Baldwin
remembered it, "when this man arranges a table, he does it
with the care and critical eye of an artist making a collage."

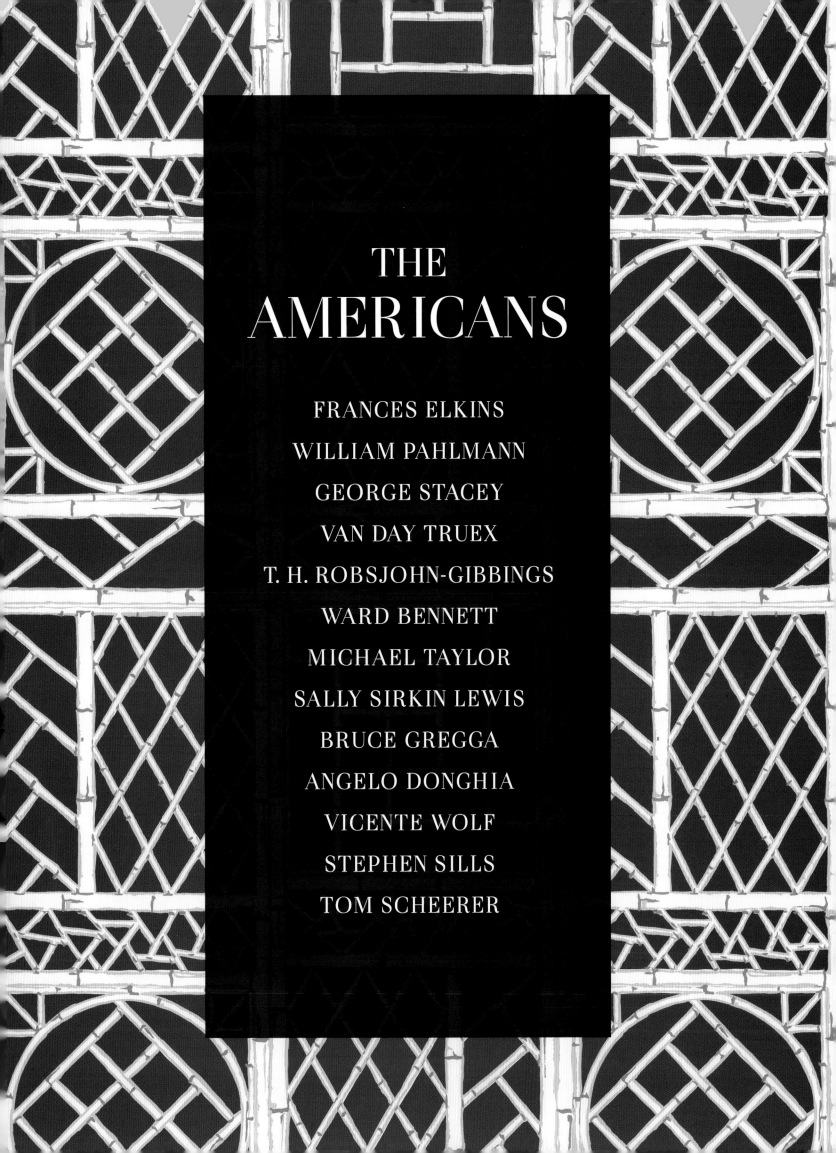

THE
AMERICANS

FRANCES ELKINS

WILLIAM PAHLMANN

GEORGE STACEY

VAN DAY TRUEX

T. H. ROBSJOHN-GIBBINGS

WARD BENNETT

MICHAEL TAYLOR

SALLY SIRKIN LEWIS

BRUCE GREGGA

ANGELO DONGHIA

VICENTE WOLF

STEPHEN SILLS

TOM SCHEERER

26 Frances Elkins
1888–1953

Feminine yet mannish; unconventional but impeccably mannered; bold while quiet—contradiction describes the work of one of America's most daring early twentieth-century decorators, Frances Elkins.

Raised in privilege in Milwaukee with her brother, the esteemed residential architect David Adler, Elkins sometimes behaved like other lady decorators of her time, showing respect for tradition with the most wholesome of furniture and fabrics. But less true to her class, Elkins also experimented with the avant-garde. In California, which she called home, and in the Chicago area, where she decorated many of the grand Lake Forest houses her brother designed, Elkins confidently translated her catholic tastes, which included French Provincial, Georgian, and French Moderne furniture, into innovative interiors. **Like the Chanel wardrobe that she wore almost exclusively, Elkins brought a sense of Continental chic to her work without losing an American lack of pretense.**

The Kersey Coates Reed house in Lake Forest was one of Elkins's (and Adler's) most famous commissions. Having befriended Jean-Michel Frank and his circle while visiting Paris, Elkins was inspired to decorate the home's library in spartan-but-sumptuous fashion: walls sheathed in tan Hermès goatskin, a leather sofa partnered with a lacquered table by Frank, and mellowed leather-bound books. It was a minimalist tour de force, and one of the most luxurious examples of early American modernism. The designer Mark Hampton deemed it "the most boldly stylish room I have ever seen in this country." And yet in the living room alongside it, the gentle furnishings included English mahogany and floral chintz more suitable to taking tea with the ladies.

Elkins's unorthodox style earned her devotion among the next generation of designers, including Michael Taylor, who, throughout his career, sung her praises: "She certainly was one of the guiding forces in the whole development of what is the American style today."

Left As Michael Taylor did decades later, Frances Elkins influenced the whole of American design with her California perspective.
Opposite Despite its chintz and outward propriety, this thirties-era Long Island living room reveals Elkins's daring in her use of a very modern Giacometti plaster lamp among the room's antiques.
Overleaf The room most identified with Elkins, the monochromatic library of the Kersey Coates Reed house (1931–1932) in Lake Forest, Illinois, featured Hermès goatskin-covered walls and a Jean-Michel Frank table.

27 | William Pahlmann
1900–1987

"As Dr. Freud has told us, there is murder in every heart, and there seems no end to the ways some clients can bedevil a decorator."

Establishing the look of the 1950s might seem a dubious distinction today, but during the mid-twentieth-century, it earned William Pahlmann high praise and recognition as America's first well-known male interior designer. **The fifties-era madness for audacious color schemes and stylistic mash-ups? We have Pahlmann to thank for that.**

"Driftwood, lime, orange, and white" was Pahlmann's self-proclaimed favorite color combination for 1954, while a few years earlier, he advocated a daring merger of "avocado, lime, plum, tan orange, and white." Once inconceivable, these color clashes were the signature of Pahlmann's bold approach, which resulted in some improbably good work. He thought nothing of combining a Japanese Shoji screen, a French Provincial desk, and contemporary vinyl flooring in rooms that could be any or all of the following: modern (such as the Swedish blond-wood furniture he popularized), traditional, or multicultural (South American crafts frequently spiced up his rooms). The designer called his freewheeling look "modern Baroque." Others called it crazy.

So how did Pahlmann spread his considerable influence, affecting the taste of an entire country? The answer lies in an early chapter of his career: as head of the decorating department at the Fifth Avenue retailer Lord & Taylor, Pahlmann is considered the first designer to have created department store model rooms. Followed closely by the public and media alike, the trendsetting rooms drew crowds eager to see Pahlmann's latest fantasies, including his now-legendary South American–inspired "Pahlmann Peruvian" rooms, visited by tens of thousands of curiosity seekers. As the designer once noted, "Decorating is one adventure that is still open to everybody."

Left The designer William Pahlmann was so prominent in his day that he was asked to pose for this 1950 Lord Calvert Whiskey Men of Distinction advertisement. **Opposite** Pahlmann was known for incorporating many different styles into one room, as in his guest bedroom, which sometimes doubled as a dining room. **Overleaf** Although better remembered for his more outré efforts, Pahlmann created many classic interiors, like this mid-century living room, which still looks good to modern eyes.

28 | George Stacey
1901–1993

"A decorator places somewhere after a psychoanalyst and a plumber—both of whom are rather more important in a crisis, although perhaps neither a psychoanalyst nor a plumber could produce an attractive interior, even in a crisis."

A maverick at the beginning of his career, an elder statesman toward the end, George Stacey made an early name for himself by redefining traditional decorating in the 1930s, taking liberties with the genteel principles established by the lady decorators.

Appealing to a new generation of socially prominent women seeking to shake things up—all three of the fabulous Cushing sisters were clients—Stacey had a style that maintained decorum but was liberated by modern flair. For socialite Frances Cheney, his lifelong patron, he crafted a Jazz Age version of Monticello, its classicism fired up by satin upholstery and mirrored flourishes. For her New York apartment, he went a step further, cloaking crown molding and door pediments in velvet and mirroring the master bedroom ceiling. Rest assured that was as risqué as Stacey ever got.

In quick time, Stacey's efforts matured into a style that was praised by subsequent generations of designers. Precise about symmetry and balance, Stacey was, as Mark Hampton described it, "constitutionally incapable of incoherent clutter and confusion." And yet Stacey never lost that flair, with gutsy strokes of primary colors made elegant by French furniture and dazzling objects—a cocktail that proved intoxicating to Princess Grace of Monaco and Ava Gardner, who both hired him. He was chic, no doubt about it, but perhaps Mario Buatta said it best: "This guy had pizzazz."

Opposite A darling of young socialites, Stacey is seen here in 1948 with client Mrs. Vincent Astor, one of the famous Cushing sisters. Left Stacey's forte was working with strong colors, which gave his work punch without overwhelming it. Overleaf Stacey's disciplined and sophisticated work at its best, in the 1950s, in the airy Palm Beach house he decorated for Blanche and Leon Levy.

29 Van Day Truex
1904–1979

"I believe in fashion, but it is a power
that can get out of hand."

Above Van Day Truex was known for almost pathological control.
Opposite Truex's tableware designs for Tiffany are now American
classics: Bamboo sterling silver flatware, Wedgwood drabware,
and the Dionysos crystal decanter.

Though not primarily a decorator, Van Day Truex was
nevertheless a central figure in American interior
design, first as head of the rigorous Parsons School of
Design and, later, as design director of Tiffany & Co. Along
with close friends Billy Baldwin and Albert Hadley, Truex
was responsible for fostering the clean, strong modern
attitude that came to define postwar American style.

The consummate Midwesterner by birth, he spent his
formative years in Paris, where he was exposed to both the
elegance of eighteenth-century French decorative arts and
the excitement of designer Jean-Michel Frank's contemporary work. From this experience, Truex cultivated an
exacting style best described by one of his frequently cited
quotations: "Control. Distill. Edit."

**His discipline was all-consuming, from the
slice of unbuttered toast he had for breakfast
every day to the perfectly balanced simplicity he
achieved through understated furnishings such
as the Parsons table** (said to be conceived at Parsons as a
class project overseen by Jean-Michel Frank and Truex), natural materials such as rattan, and most of all, the color beige.
Truex was so enamored of it Baldwin quipped, "Someday
Van is going to beige himself to death." Modern and minimal, Truex's taste broadened the more traditional perspective of Baldwin and, later, informed the forward-looking
sensibility of Albert Hadley, who was his student at Parsons.
"I think about the future," Hadley once said. "I learned this
from Van Truex." It was Truex who introduced Hadley to
Sister Parish, thus creating this country's most illustrious
design firm, Parish-Hadley Associates.

Truex's steady hand proved especially fruitful during
his tenure at Tiffany & Co. After banishing the retailer's
more commonplace offerings—fussy china patterns were
his bête noire—Truex refined the Tiffany aesthetic, introducing Bamboo sterling silver flatware, accessories simu-
lating rock crystal, and Wedgwood drabware place settings,
all of which remain highly collectible today. Now considered classics, his Tiffany designs represent a high-water
mark in the history of American taste.

Having spent his life paring his style down to a minimum, the ever-chic Truex needed little more than Brunschwig & Fils's Les Touches fabric and a few Parsons tables in his final New York City apartment.

30 | T. H. Robsjohn-Gibbings
1905–1976

> "For one interior that gives delight, there are starved purer-than-thou pretentious 'modern' rooms with wall-to-wall social frustration or a new gluttonous decor (gracious camp) that suggests a head-up plate of rijsttafel."

Opposite At the end of his life, Robsjohn-Gibbings settled in Athens; a chaise longue version of his iconic klismos chair for Saridis provided a perch among the ruins. **Above** A departure from his earlier, far more dramatic efforts, Robsjohn-Gibbings's mid-century work, with its classical lines and blond woods, was a highly personal interpretation of the times. **Overleaf** A furniture designer and decorator, Robsjohn-Gibbings wore both hats at Casa Encantada, the Bel Air, California, estate built in the late 1930s—the pinnacle of his early work.

Inspiration strikes in unexpected places. For English-born designer, T. H. Robsjohn-Gibbings, it was the British Museum, where his study of Ancient Greek vase paintings sparked a novel idea: to adapt the furniture depicted on these millennia-old vases for a modern audience. Recognizing the simplicity of the Ancient Greek aesthetic as a model for pared-down contemporary living, the Londoner decamped to Manhattan, where he opened a showroom to promote his groundbreaking collection of classically inspired furnishings, including what would become his signature piece: the klismos chair, which he considered "perhaps the most beautiful chair ever made."

The showroom's success spurred a spate of decorating assignments for Gibby, as he was known. His early efforts were, frankly, tinged with thirties-era pastiche. But by the 1940s and 1950s, his work became simpler and better suited to the mid-century modernist houses that were taking America by storm. So, too, were his furniture designs, their blond wood and sleek surfaces echoing the increasingly popular Scandinavian style.

Inventive yes, irascible definitely, Robsjohn-Gibbings gained acclaim for his 1944 book, *Good-bye, Mr. Chippendale*. A biting takedown of the cult of antique furniture—"As far as I am concerned, the sooner the collapse comes the better," he wrote—the book gleefully skewered anyone associated with the antiques business as crooks, including dealers and lady decorators, with poor Dorothy Draper receiving a heaping of scorn. Reserving praise for contemporary design, the designer nevertheless managed to slip in accolades for his beloved Ancient Greek furniture. He went on to write two more howlers: *Mona Lisa's Moustache: A Dissection of Modern Art* (1947) and *Homes of the Brave* (1954).

Highly opinionated and vocal, Gibby firmly believed in what he preached, eventually moving to the source of his life's work, Athens. There, at the end of his life, while making his most beautifully crafted furniture yet with the local firm Saridis, he also created his greatest and most beguiling achievement: an apartment of breathtaking simplicity, overlooking the Acropolis.

31 | Ward Bennett
1917–2003

"In life and design, try to pull it all down to a minimum."

Ward Bennett's life was one big adventure. He dropped out of school at a young age and moved from job to job. He studied under the sculptor Constantin Brâncuși, shared studio space with the artist Louise Nevelson, and designed clothing under the Hattie Carnegie label. But his most defining achievement was as a designer of interiors and furniture, becoming one of America's foremost champions of modern minimalism.

He was a renegade in fifties-era Manhattan. **"I want to limit, to simplify"—and he meant business, distilling rooms to their essence and incorporating furniture into architecture, literally.** Bennett is considered the originator of the conversation pit, a mid-century novelty that was stylish when executed by him, if not so much by others. Bennett's work was so exciting for its time it won the recognition of Gianni and Marella Agnelli, who hired him to decorate their Rome apartment. The couturier Hubert de Givenchy exclaimed upon first viewing its travertine-clad entrance hall and unadorned windows and doors, "This is the only contemporary house I have seen that has true grandeur."

Bennett's choice of materials was especially cutting-edge, foreshadowing the high-tech look that swept the 1970s. He introduced industrial elements into residential spaces: subway grating as a windowsill, for example, or his famous I-beam table, taking its cue from the new glass skyscrapers of the time. The resulting rooms were assertively modern, but never cold or antiseptic. No place was this better illustrated than in his own apartment, cobbled together from former maids' rooms in the garret of Manhattan's most celebrated apartment building, the Dakota. Monastic, indulgent, strict, disciplined, and cozy at the same time, it was a landmark in interior design—arguably the most exciting modern apartment in New York in its day.

Left Throughout his career, Ward Bennett made it a point not to get locked into "one narrow category." **Opposite** Bennett's Manhattan apartment, cobbled together in the Dakota attic, captured his architectural approach at its most spectacular in one of the city's most memorable interiors. **Overleaf** The softer country version of Bennett style, in his home in East Hampton, New York.

32 | Michael Taylor
1927–1986

> "Diana Vreeland called me the 'Jimmy Dean of the decorating world.' I was a rebel."

A trailblazer who went where no designer had ever before ventured, Michael Taylor, the San Francisco legend whose daring new approach to American design became a dominant look of the 1970s, explained his motive this way: "I was young, I was in California, and it was time, many of us here felt, for a fresh approach to decorating."

His early work shows traces of Frances Elkins, from whom Taylor adopted the freedom to experiment with a variety of styles, and Syrie Maugham, whose all-white period set the tone for the designer's career. By the early 1970s, however, Taylor was working entirely within an idiom of his own, one that brought the outdoors inside. An organic, bleached palette was all his, as were rugged, natural materials like slate, wood logs, and stone, which the designer often had fabricated into tables that were so heavy they sometimes required cranes to hoist them indoors.

Two more hallmarks of Taylor's later work that will always be associated with the designer: huge chairs and sofas upholstered in white or cream, accented with cannonball throw pillows; and basket-shod trees placed indoors, which took the decorating world by storm. **Earthy yet discerning, this revolutionary California Look, as it was dubbed, captured all the cultural currents of the 1970s.**

Although created for his California clientele and their spacious, light-filled houses, Taylor's work proved highly influential elsewhere, even in the urban jungle of New York City, where he set tongues wagging with his work on socialite Nan Kemper's Park Avenue duplex. In its drawing room, Taylor combined elegant Coromandel screens with banquettes covered in corduroy, a high-low mix that was so bewitching Kempner claimed, "Every decorator in town tried to come in and knock it off."

Above In an effort to "start from scratch," Michael Taylor created an entirely new genre in American design: the California Look, which emphasized "the white floor, the white wall, the perfect plant." **Opposite** At the heart of Taylor's style were organic elements like wicker furniture, stone floors, indoor trees, and even tree-trunk beds, here on display at his San Francisco office. **Overleaf** Taylor's interiors consistently blurred the boundary between indoors and out, perhaps nowhere more dramatically than in the Malibu, California, home he designed for Mr. and Mrs. Stanley Beyer in 1971.

33 | Sally Sirkin Lewis

1932–

"One thing that is paramount
in my work is quietude."

The most prominent woman among the 1970s-era Californians who found fame via the pages of the increasingly influential *Architectural Digest*—she would go on to decorate editor in chief Paige Rense's own house—Los Angeles–based Sally Sirkin Lewis **married West and East Coast sensibilities into a sophisticated look that she trademarked through her J. Robert Scott line of furniture and textiles.**

"For myself, I don't like an explicitly 'California' look," she said. "I don't dress that way; never owned a pair of jeans in my life." Aspects of Lewis's work referenced the relaxed, California lifestyle: white cotton sofas, banquettes, and chaises, as lounge-worthy as a Malibu beach house, frequented her projects. But at some point they always took a serious turn. A graphic color palette would add a dose of drama. Contrasting textures and finishes would add polish and vigor. "I don't like anything weak," said Lewis. "I like clarity and strength."

Less infatuated with the organic elements that captivated most of her California colleagues, Lewis showed a preference instead for high-style decorations, especially Art Deco furniture and Japanese decorative arts. She combined both interests in her own Beverly Hills living room, its walls painted to mimic a Japanese screen. Unlike anything anybody had ever seen, the room led to a brief craze for the crane motif and remains one of the most memorable interiors ever depicted in *Architectural Digest*.

Left Sally Sirkin Lewis's confident style earned her an impressive clientele that included Ali MacGraw and Joni Mitchell.
Opposite Lewis's own Beverly Hills living room, with its crane motif against gold-leaf tea paper splendor, was arguably the most memorable interior published in *Architectural Digest*.

34 | Bruce Gregga
1933–

"I like a few important pieces, not a lot of things."

Coco Chanel was referring to fashion when she uttered her famous line, "Elegance is refusal," but she could have just as easily been describing the work of Bruce Gregga. **He has spent a lifetime championing a highly personal view of restraint and luxury,** from his professional roots in Chicago to his long career in Los Angeles (where he lived in a John Woolf–designed cottage on Hollywood film director George Cukor's estate) to his current life in Montecito, where he is proprietor of a beloved antiques shop, William Laman.

"One of the mistakes ... of the earlier modernists was their strongly held belief that the accumulation of intricate and richly associative objects was some sort of social lapse," Gregga believes. So he found his own approach to modernism, paring down his rooms while, at the same time, enriching them. The architecture of a Gregga interior was, more often than not, a box, devoid of trim and molding: "You stand more of a chance of achieving the desired impact if you're not competing with plaster wreaths or painted garlands." But what little decoration he permitted was of exceptional quality. It often included contemporary upholstered seating, antique French chairs, Coromandel screens, Asian or European porcelains, and sensual fabrics like satin, silk, and fur. In a Gregga interior, there was never a trace of black leather or chrome.

One of the most interesting parts of Gregga's career was his early work as a set designer for the fashion photographer Victor Skrebneski, who shot Estée Lauder's famed magazine advertisements in the 1970s and '80s. Distinctive for posh backdrops that were fully furnished down to their ashtrays, many of the ads were photographed in Skrebneski's Chicago home, designed with Gregga's assistance. The ad campaign proved so captivating admirers were known to copy Gregga's settings in their own homes.

Left After making a name for himself in Chicago during the 1970s, Bruce Gregga decamped to California and quickly became one of the West Coast's leading designers. **Opposite** Gregga has a unique way of marrying modern architecture and furnishings with refined antiques, like the French examples in this Chicago high-rise. **Overleaf** "I like a house to have a quiet feel to it," which Gregga creates by allowing room for furniture to breathe.

35 Angelo Donghia
1935–1985

"Too many people treat decorating like an art form. It's not. Decorating is a business."

Angelo Donghia, the superstar of the 1970s, **sensualized modernism for the most self-indulgent of decades**, turning away from the hard edges of chrome and glass. Like his California counterpart, Michael Taylor, he became known for oversize furniture so voluptuously padded it was labeled "fluffy" by its creator and "superstuffed" by others. Often based on frames that recalled Jean-Michel Frank's designs, but with bun feet, Donghia's furniture sparked a renewed appreciation for Frank. No less striking was Donghia's affinity for finishes and colors that looked their most ravishing at night, when lit dramatically. Silver-foil or gold tea-paper ceilings, a Champagne palette, and pale wood floors typically set the mood in a Donghia interior, along with tactile fabrics, like satin and gray flannel suiting. The designer used the latter so lavishly he was referred to as "the man in the gray flannel sofa."

Much like Donghia's frequent haunt, Studio 54, his interiors were symbols of a particular moment in Manhattan. His ultimate validation was work for two of that decade's most influential and exacting taste makers, Ralph Lauren and Halston. Yet despite his strong, recognizable style, he could be astonishingly versatile: Donald Trump's gilded Trump Tower apartment is credited to him.

Perhaps more than any other designer, Donghia possessed extraordinary business acumen. "I deal in the mass market and in the class market," he would say. He diversified into to-the-trade fabrics and furniture, as well as mass-market bedding and tableware. The designer's efforts were so successful that when he died of AIDS in 1985—the most high-profile New York designer to succumb at that point—his company was already a multimillion-dollar luxury conglomerate. It is still going strong today.

Left In both design and business, Angelo Donghia was always two steps ahead of everyone, even accurately predicting that designer showrooms would someday be open to the public. **Opposite** Donghia received reams of publicity for his Key West, Florida, beach house, which was purchased by Calvin Klein in 1980.

For Ralph Lauren's Fifth Avenue apartment, the designer fearlessly stripped away the prewar details and created one of Manhattan's most unforgettable interiors: stark white furniture with a view of Central Park.

36 Vicente Wolf

1946–

"It's taken a long time for Americans to become aware that simplicity can be elaborate."

Vicente Wolf tried his hand at merchandising, banking, and modeling before eventually joining interior designer Bob Patino to form Patino/Wolf Associates, one of Manhattan's hottest firms of the 1970s and '80s. It was a very sexy time, the disco era, and they were at the center of it, channeling the provocative attitudes of that era with carpeted platforms and—famously, in their own apartment—leather sectionals on wheels that would go skating around their living room. Every time you visited, the room would be rearranged.

But Wolf gained acclaim for taking a softer, more organic approach to modernism at a time when it was completely stark. At the helm of his own firm since the late 1980s, Wolf has maintained his mellow point of view, describing his solo work as "more relaxed, more human and livable."

"The thread is whiteness," he says. "It holds everything together." White walls, upholstery, and slipcovers create Zen-like environments that give "the sense that everything is surrounded by air." Wolf's other great contribution has been the liberties he has taken with furniture placement, especially his trademark: an oversize, framed mirror casually leaning against a wall. That one seemingly small gesture has trickled down to boutique hotels and furniture catalogues around the world. And yet it's never all purely modern; there's also an antique or two in every Wolf room: "I am a true believer in the sense of spaces that have an elegant classic sense without compromising modern integrity."

Wolf was one of the first designers to use black-and-white photography in his interiors, at a time when it was still a poor cousin to painting. Long passionate about it, Wolf has in recent years become a photographer of note himself, with exhibitions and books. He says, "It took me a long time to realize that I'm not just a guy who places furniture."

Left Still a central figure in contemporary design, Vicente Wolf recalls, "When I started in the 1970s, modernism was completely stark." **Opposite** The designer's New York City loft summarizes the Wolf look: furniture placed on the diagonal, a mirror propped on the floor, black-and-white photography, and an abundance of white.

37 | Stephen Sills
1951–

"It costs a lot more money to look subtle."

Despite having decorated for a roster of famous clients, the project for which Stephen Sills will always be remembered is, ironically, his own small Manhattan apartment. Published frequently in a number of publications beginning in the late 1980s, it stopped the decorating world in its tracks, in part because of its custom fluted plaster molding and cobblestone flooring, but mostly because of its powerful, tranquil atmosphere. It did wonders for Sills's career, propelling the boy from Oklahoma—and his then-partner, the designer James Huniford—to the heights of the international design world. His admirers have included fashion designer Vera Wang, *Vogue*'s career-making editor Anna Wintour, and the notoriously discerning couturier Karl Lagerfeld, who deemed Sills's own Bedford, New York, house "the chicest house in America."

Sills helped sweep away the excesses of 1980s decorating, establishing a classical-yet-modern style that he described as "kind of underdecorated, but with fabulous objects." At first glance, the backdrops of Sills's pared-down settings look simple enough, but appearances can be deceiving. Those seemingly uncomplicated biscuit-colored paint shades and classically inspired architectural finishes require a great deal of highly skilled labor, not to mention cash, to achieve.

And then there is the outstanding furniture that has come to define a Sills interior, be it the twenty-one-piece suite of gilded Louis Philippe furniture he installed in Tina Turner's house in the South of France or priceless furniture of more recent vintage, such as the Jean-Michel Frank pieces that fit so well with his work. Chasing down the heels of down-filled, silk-covered sofas swamped by passementerie, Sills's work might have offered an alternative to visual excess, but—truth be told—proved just as expensive.

Left Sills and then-partner James Huniford gained early acclaim when photos of their New York apartment, seen here, made the rounds among the high-end magazines.
Opposite A bracing relief after the overwrought 1980s, Stephen Sills's work brought back serenity and elegance.

The designer's own house
in Bedford, New York, is a
sophisticated puzzle of stately
materials, complex finishes,
and blue-chip furniture.

38 | Tom Scheerer
1955–

> "I'd rather leave a job slightly underbaked . . . 'No, let's *not* do the four hundred silhouettes on the wall of the powder room.'"

Reeking of confidence and seemingly impervious to trends, Tom Scheerer is like the proverbial box of chocolates: you never know what you're going to get, but it's always delicious.

Bentwood chairs, Noguchi paper lanterns, and preppy wallpapers might seem to make strange bedfellows, but all three appear with some frequency in his work. A decoupaged chest here. An oval laminate Saarinen table there. His work is undoubtedly eclectic, yet he is the last person who would thumb his nose at tradition. Like Nancy Lancaster and Sister Parish before him, Scheerer spent a privileged childhood in surroundings that instilled in him a strong understanding of a well-run house, as well as the notion that a house should never look like it's trying too hard. No-nonsense and not inclined to grand—and especially grandiose—gestures, Scheerer brings a relaxed, all-American sensibility to his clients' homes, endowing them with a fresh-looking mix of tried-and-true classics that project nonchalance, always with a surprise.

Despite his best intentions, however, the designer's work invariably ends up making quite an impression. No Scheerer project has earned more fanfare than his ravishing overhaul of the Lyford Cay Club in the Bahamas. Its Chippendale lattice, pinks and greens, repurposed furniture, and chocolate-brown grass cloth walls hand-painted with seventeen-foot-tall palm trees are quintessential Scheerer. Discovered by magazines and social media, the secretive club's interiors became legendary practically overnight in 2011. Although he described Lyford as "a living and breathing Slim Aarons world," he could just as easily have been referring to his own work, whose old guard roots have been reenergized for today.

Left The most American of American designers, Tom Scheerer admits, "Formality is not my thing." Opposite Scheerer is unique in his affection for bentwood chairs, which he uses often, here in unlikely combination with scenic wallpaper. Overleaf Scheerer's makeover of the Lyford Cay Club, with stenciled grass cloth walls, was such photographic gold it caused a social media meltdown. It's a room that will be remembered.

THE ENGLISH MASTERS

MRS. GUY BETHELL

BASIL IONIDES

NANCY LANCASTER

JOHN FOWLER

GEOFFREY BENNISON

JOHN STEFANIDIS

NICHOLAS HASLAM

DAVID MLINARIC

NINA CAMPBELL

ROBERT KIME

VEERE GRENNEY

KIT KEMP

BEN PENTREATH

39 | The Hon. Mrs. Guy (Ethel) Bethell

1865–1932

The English country house style owes a debt of gratitude to the Hon. Mrs. Guy Bethell, one of the great ladies who were decorating stately homes well before the prominence of Colefax & Fowler, indeed when decorating was hardly considered a profession. As co-owner of Elden Ltd., the Mayfair firm she founded in 1904, Bethell was a leading source of the chintzes and other fine fabrics that graced many country houses. **She made an indelible impression on both John Fowler and Nancy Lancaster, both of whom cited her influence throughout their careers.**

With a flair for color not unlike that of Fowler, Bethell was as adept working with a symphony of whites as she was with saturated hues. Some speculate that it was her novel way of lacquering strong colors that might have inspired Fowler's choice of wall finish for Lancaster's legendary yellow drawing room. Yet she herself was rather self-possessed, her restraint resulting in rooms of remarkable sophistication. Which is to say, she knew when to stop.

Though scant evidence remains of her work, a few of her efforts have been preserved in photographs, most notably her work at Kelmarsh Hall, the home of Nancy Lancaster. In addition to supplying fabrics and curtains, Bethell was also responsible for decorating Lancaster's own bedroom, a chic ensemble of ivory damask and silver lamé, as well as the Exhibition Bedroom, so named for the 1927 decorating event for which the room's furnishings were originally created. Visiting the exhibition, Lancaster was so taken with Bethell's apricot-colored brocade bed hangings, ivory taffeta curtains, and hand-painted floral pelmet she bought it all. A fan for life, Lancaster later said that Bethell was "by far the best decorator I have ever known."

Below Nancy Lancaster engaged Mrs. Bethell to furnish her Kelmarsh Hall bedroom, a shimmering affair that included ivory damask bed hangings trimmed with silver lamé. Opposite Like her admirer John Fowler, Bethell handled complex color schemes with aplomb, as in this stippled-green London drawing room captured in a William Ranken illustration.

40 Basil Ionides
1884–1950

"A crimson door is an abomination."

Prominent during the Art Deco period, Basil Ionides helped define the glamour of 1920's London, with his work on the Savoy Theatre, its silver-leafed and gold-lacquered auditorium regarded as a Deco tour de force, as well as the still-fashionable Claridge's hotel. Less lauded, though no less significant, was the designer's role in selecting the finishes and decor for Mrs. Winkie Philipson's house, Encombe, whose whitewashed, bleached-out interiors are thought to have inspired Syrie Maugham and her famous all-white music room.

Ionides won his greatest acclaim as a color theorist with his groundbreaking 1926 book, *Colour and Interior Decoration.* One of the most opinionated design manuals ever written, it provided explicit instructions on working with color, light, and appropriate decorations, which were detailed in charts and illustrations. Mapping out "Decorative Schemes in Blue"—take a deep breath—Ionides suggested a sitting room with walls painted deep Wedgwood blue, accompanied by a matte parchment-colored ceiling, black floor, mauve Samarkand rug, curtains of a Chinese-patterned cretonne, orange and yellow taffeta cushions, and Oriental-figure lamps crowned by orange lampshades.

He was unusually confident when making big color pronouncements. "Pink and gold are apt to cloy," he wrote, "but a little gold with pink is effective." Silver, however, requires caution: "Silver is pleasant but needs great care not to become morbid." Who could argue with that?

Below For the drawing room of Howbridge Hall in Essex, England, Ionides concocted a color scheme comprised almost entirely of shades of pink, as illustrated in his 1926 book, *Colour and Interior Decoration.* Opposite Ionides dazzled London with his Art Deco treatment of the Savoy Theatre, which was restored to its former glory in the 1990s.

41 | Nancy Lancaster
1897–1994

"I can't bear anything that looks like it's been decorated."

How did an American make the cut in a chapter about the English masters? Unique in the history of design, Nancy Lancaster of Virginia spent most of her life in England, applied American notions of comfort to the country house tradition, and hatched a new style of undecorated English decorating that set the standard for the English.

The faded elegance of Lancaster's ancestral home, Mirador, informed her work throughout her life in England, where she settled in 1926. Over the course of two marriages she rescued, modernized, and created landmarks of traditional decorating at Kelmarsh Hall, Ditchley Park, and Haseley Court. She brandished color like a sword, had an eye for the singular object, could jumble mementos and effects to make a newly decorated room appear assembled over time, and would do whatever necessary to achieve her ends, including tea-staining and sun-bleaching fabrics. Her great revolution was her introduction of the en suite bathroom and American plumbing, which helped to turn intimidating, miserably cold houses into symbols of coziness and comfort. And thus, the English country house style was born.

Nobody else in decorating history created so many unforgettable rooms: the unheard-of pink hall at Kelmarsh, meant to play up the red coats of riders after a hunt; the dreamlike Tobacco Bedroom at Haseley Court, with its sepia and ivory wallpaper mural; and possibly the most reproduced room ever, the "buttah-yellah" drawing room (Lancaster never lost her Southern drawl) over the Colefax & Fowler shop, where she lived until the end of her life. By her side through it all was John Fowler, her partner at their esteemed English decorating firm, Colefax & Fowler, which Lancaster purchased from founder Sibyl Colefax in 1944. A petulant union that earned them the moniker "the most unhappy unmarried couple in England," the partners were nevertheless simpatico, and took each other to the pinnacle of their profession.

Opposite Nancy Lancaster placed as much importance on her houses' gardens as she did on their interiors. **Left** For the Gothic Bedroom at Haseley Court, Lancaster asked John Fowler and the decorative painter George Oakes to create the illusion of stucco ornamentation on the ceiling. Even she was fooled by their painterly efforts, exclaiming, "Damn, John, it's stucco and not trompe l'oeil."

Lancaster's butter-
yellow drawing room,
above Colefax & Fowler's
former Brook Street
premises, is perhaps the
best-loved room in the
history of design. In fact
it resembled no known
shade of butter.

42 | John Fowler
1906–1977

"I like the decoration of a room to be . . .
mannered, yet casual and unselfconscious."

Above Nancy Lancaster once said of her partner, "John Fowler
has 'it,' whatever 'it' is." **Opposite** With his perfect pitch for color,
Fowler conceived a complex paint scheme with twelve shades of
white for the Great Hall at Syon House, the London home of the
Duke of Northumberland. **Overleaf** In the 1950s, Fowler had
the walls of the drawing room at Hambleden painted a strong
pink, knowing that over time, they would mellow to the attractive
shade of apricot seen here.

Not to the manor born, John Fowler nevertheless perfected the art of decorating the manor, honing his design skills first as a partner with Sibyl Colefax and, later, Nancy Lancaster. Famous for setting each other's teeth on edge, Fowler and Lancaster nonetheless proved to be formidable. Whereas Lancaster relied on instinct, Fowler was the cerebral of the two, applying his authoritative knowledge of history and his superior technical skills to their work. Together, they brought the country house into the twentieth century, enlivening their interiors with what Fowler coined "humble elegance"—the very essence of English style.

Fowler impressed a light touch upon his work. Eighteenth-century French furniture, a favorite of his, and painted furniture leavened the brown woods preferred by previous generations. Trompe l'oeil—his signature Venetian blind chintz, or the drapery-motif wallpaper by the French firm Mauny—also lent charm.

But Fowler was dead-serious when it came to his construction of curtains, whose success has yet to be repeated. Having studied eighteenth-century costume, Fowler cut impeccably proportioned fancy-dress curtains that were decorating's equivalent of a couturier's work.

His other great achievement was his masterful way with color and painted effects. **Whether replicating long-lost paint colors for the National Trust, layering colors until the result matched what was in his head, balancing pretty colors with muddy ones to create his signature undecorated look, or simply concocting clever names for subtle colors that are his and his alone—mouse's back and dead salmon—Fowler worked tirelessly to devise exacting color schemes with extraordinarily complex pigments.**

Fastidious though he was, Fowler loosened up considerably when decorating his own country house, the Hunting Lodge in Hampshire. It might not have been grand, but it was charming and certainly his most-loved project—the quintessential example of humble elegance.

Left The sitting room of the Hunting Lodge, Fowler's beloved country house, was an intriguing combination of color, from the Sienna-pink walls and vibrant yellow chair down to the carpet, in a shade Fowler called "dead mouse." Above Everything about the Hunting Lodge spoke to Fowler's fondness for "humble elegance."

43 | Geoffrey Bennison
1921–1984

> "What most people expect of a decorator—ghastly good taste and period pedantry—is anathema to me."

One of England's legendary dealer-decorators, Geoffrey Bennison parlayed an early career selling antiques from a stall on Portobello Road in the 1950s into the role of internationally acclaimed designer. **The impish Bennison was the most theatrical of English decorators**; even the extravagant *le goût Rothschild* paled in comparison.

"Something mad on top of something very good, or something very good on top of something mad" was how Bennison once described his work, though it was more nuanced than that. Indeed, what could have been madder than the large carved camel in Bennison's own London flat? And yet a Bennison interior was never campy. As the designer used to say, "No cherubs, dear."

A romantic ambience was at the heart of the Bennison style. Nothing could be more English in spirit than his own extensive fabric line, which offers a "time-faded" as well as a full-strength version of many fabrics. They mixed beautifully with antique textiles and exotic tokens, such as Turkish carpets and Chinese porcelains, to create Bennison's distinctive style. He also displayed a remarkable command of complex colors, honed during his student days at the prestigious Slade School of Art. With its rich, deep hues like terracotta, Prussian blue, and something the designer called Red Riding Hood Red, his palette required such a deft touch few other designers dared to attempt it.

Bennison's work was exclusive and expensive, and he chose only those projects that interested him. His elite clientele, which included Jordanian royalty as well as Rothschilds, was known as "the happy few."

Opposite Photographed in 1981, Geoffrey Bennison holds court in his legendary Pimlico Road shop, surrounded by the rich fabrics and distinctive antiques for which he is best remembered.
Left Highly selective of his clients, Bennison assembled this lavish Paris apartment for Baron David de Rothschild.
Overleaf Less grand, though no less ravishing, was Bennison's Mayfair apartment in London, its living room painted his signature shade of Red Riding Hood Red.

44 | John Stefanidis

1937–

"Decorating a house is not about following received opinion. Taste should reflect your spirit."

Born to Greek parents in Alexandria, Egypt, schooled at Oxford, and based in Milan before eventually moving to London, **John Stefanidis is the most cosmopolitan of British designers.**

As polished as the designer himself—Stefanidis is a frequent presence on the International Best-Dressed List—his interiors always have a sense of appropriateness, owing in part to work that "changes according to the climate." When decorating the headquarters of the Bank of England or the country house of the Duke of Westminster, Stefanidis crafts spaces that are the very essence of English propriety. And yet, the exotic is often lurking in his rooms, brought there by the worldly souvenirs that Stefanidis favors, such as Ottoman-inspired textiles. "I do so many different moods," Stefanidis said, something that has allowed the designer to cultivate an international clientele. As acclaimed as his work may be, however, he maintains that slight English embarrassment with decorating as a whole: "When I finish a room, it should look as though it has had nothing done to it."

When not working in England, Stefanidis is likely to be found on Patmos, the Greek island to which he has retreated for decades. Something of a local legend there, Stefanidis has spent the last fifty years luring friends to the island and designing their houses (including one for Prince Sadruddin Aga Khan), which have helped to make Patmos a popular destination for the rich and famous. His style of island decorating—think bleached earthiness quenched by vivid colors, blue especially—is every bit as sophisticated as his work back home and has an entire book devoted to it: *An Island Sanctuary: A House in Greece.*

Left John Stefanidis is like his interiors: worldly, and the quintessential English gentleman. **Opposite** Stefanidis works in many styles, always tailored to its location; for this London interior, the look is classic English.

Stefanidis has become
almost synonymous with the
Greek island of Patmos, where
his relaxed, breezy island style
is in high demand.

45 Nicholas Haslam
1939–

"My designs are like very stylish women. They are smart, couture, and polished."

With the many personas he has assumed over the years—you never know if he will show up in a finely cut suit or with his hair in spikes like a 1980s punk off the King's Road—Nicholas "Nicky" Haslam is England's design chameleon, cloaking interiors in tweedy respectability one day, Imperial Russian opulence the next. **Whatever the mood, there's a fizzy quality that has been a constant through all his work.** A Haslam room is a glass of Champagne.

Born in Buckinghamshire, he spent his twenties in America, where he worked for *Vogue*, befriended an unknown Andy Warhol, socialized with Cole Porter, and passed a spell on an Arizona horse ranch. He explains: "By English standards, my work has a very American look. The taste is English but there's an American style to it."

In Haslam's world, comfort is a given, but always updated from the "scruffiness we English are so proud of." His flair for theatrics, reminiscent of Cecil Beaton, dates from his Eton days, when he decorated his room in flamboyant "barococo-surreal." Whether faux-finishing panels of ordinary fiberboard to imitate elegant wood paneling or sheathing closet doors in Vuitton leather, Haslam never hesitates to "mock things up like a stage set."

Decorating—for clients like the musician Bryan Ferry, Princess Michael of Kent, and too many Russians to name—is only part of the Haslam story. He has been a fixture in the social pages of newspapers and magazines for decades. He has had gigs as a singer and cabaret performer. And he is a very clever writer, with a newspaper column, "How Common!," that gleefully savaged all things naff, and a well-received 2009 memoir, *Redeeming Features*, to his name.

Opposite In this recent photograph, Nicky Haslam stands in his London home, in a pose only he could strike. **Left** Now the proud inhabitant of the Hunting Lodge, John Fowler's former country house, Haslam has changed the scale but very much preserved the spirit. **Overleaf** One of Haslam's closest friends is the singer and onetime Roxy Music front man Bryan Ferry, for whom Haslam decorated this surprisingly traditional drawing room in London in the 1980s.

46 | David Mlinaric
1939–

"People often overstate the case. So much of decoration is just over the top."

Considered the late twentieth-century successor to John Fowler, David Mlinaric was his country's foremost practitioner of traditional decorating as well as an expert on historical restoration. But unlike Fowler, with his eighteenth-century perspective, the now-retired Mlinaric mastered a range of styles over the course of his career.

"Decoration should be in response to the architecture," he once said. That might mean ornate Gothic wallpaper for an eighteenth-century Irish country house, or Diego Giacometti furniture and traditional English matting for a Loire Valley château. The one constant throughout was a steadfast opposition to showy effects, nowhere more splendidly on display than in his own Somerset country house, with its deceptively skillful, relaxed furniture arrangement under a Rex Whistler oil painting. Mlinaric was so against showing off that he even declined to write his own monograph so that he could avoid using the word "I."

Clients such as Mick Jagger and Lord Jacob Rothschild marked his distinctive career, but he was also frequently called upon to consult on the restoration of England's greatest buildings, often under the aegis of the National Trust. Mlinaric's preservation work has included the Assembly Rooms in Bath, known far and wide to Jane Austen fans, and Spencer House, the eighteenth-century London house of Earl Spencer.

Left Known for designing some of England's most magnificent houses, David Mlinaric has never lost perspective, once saying, "Only a family can keep a house alive." **Opposite** When restoring the Yellow Breakfast Room at Nostell Priory in Yorkshire, Mlinaric hewed to the house's eighteenth-century origins, reproducing a wallpaper and damask from the era. **Overleaf** Compared with his work for the National Trust, the designer's own country home, Spargrove in Somerset, is decidedly less grand but no less sophisticated.

47 | Nina Campbell
1945–

"The English don't decorate as often or as thoroughly as the Americans. If a set of curtains were worn, John Fowler would dye the borders and add a tassel tieback. That works here, but not everywhere."

A former assistant to John Fowler, Nina Campbell might have been schooled in the best English country houses, but throughout her long career, she has never succumbed to their self-sacrificing spartan quality. Campbell has said of these venerable country houses: "The reality is, you get pneumonia and they're not very comfortable."

She had a cosmopolitan upbringing in London, which nurtured a style that is urbane and polished, and might explain why Campbell's brand of English decor translates easily to other countries. **America in particular appreciates her work's sparkle and tidiness,** and that has earned Campbell a loyal following on these shores. It may lack the expected measure of shabbiness, but neither does it look too new—she is English, after all. "There is a knack in England for giving things a lived-in look," says Campbell. "Little bits and pieces that are funny or scrappy and loved give a room a lived-in feel."

Her interiors often have a clubby feel to them, and indeed many such establishments have engaged Campbell to create or make over their interiors. One of Campbell's earliest and best-known projects was the interior of Annabel's, the legendary London nightclub. Designed to make guests look their best, Annabel's was, in the words of Campbell, "smart, but never stuffy," a sentiment that could just as easily describe the whole of Campbell's work.

Above "Comfortable" sums up every project of Nina Campbell's. She says, "It's terribly important to feel at home."
Opposite Although the members-only London nightclub Annabel's recently moved, its former location was celebrated for its Campbell-designed interiors, including the red-lacquered Buddha Room. **Overleaf** The designer's own home in London illustrates Campbell's polished-yet-cozy style.

48 | Robert Kime
1946–

"The house always has the last word. But I always have the first word."

Calling the Prince of Wales a client would be enough of an achievement for any designer, but for Robert Kime, it is but one of many. A master of traditional English decorating, often with currents of the Middle East and Orientalism, Kime is at the very top of his profession, both at home and abroad.

He has been called upon to decorate some of Britain's finest houses. At Clarence House, Prince Charles asked the designer to freshen his grandmother's former home. Yet Kime is also in demand by rock royalty, having decorated South Wraxall Manor, the Wiltshire home of Duran Duran guitarist John Taylor and his wife, Gela, the founder of Juicy Couture. Kime's introduction of tapestries, camel back sofas, and antique carpets to this quintessential country setting has made it one of the most photographed English houses in recent memory.

Arguably the heir to Geoffrey Bennison, Kime is at his very best with his exotic fabrics, on display at his London shop along with antiques and reproduction lines suitable for filling in an earl's family seat. And yet despite his very English calculated eccentricity, Kime—unlike Bennison—avoids theatricality and grandeur. Unassuming, cozy, and not prone to spectacle, Kime's work is the twenty-first-century model for aristocratic English reserve.

Left Robert Kime believes that "provided the proportions are right, a room should work, whether it's for a gardener or the Queen of Spain." **Opposite** Kime is highly regarded for his line of fabrics, which are based on his collection of antique textiles, often from the Middle East. **Overleaf** Kime's distinctly loose style of decorating is evident in the designer's own sitting room, in his house in Wiltshire, England. "I absolutely hate over-controlled decoration."

49 | Veere Grenney

1949–

"History of decoration in England is different because one isn't so worried about everything going together."

As a former director of Colefax & Fowler, New Zealand–born Veere Grenney could be expected to revel in well-mannered chintzes and cheerful colors. Think again. They might remain a part of his vocabulary—he maintains a special fondness for Colefax & Fowler's most famous chintz, *Bowood*—but since establishing his own highly successful firm, **Veere Grenney has succeeded in giving English decorating a thorough cleansing, in turn introducing a new breed of English style.**

The noticeable difference is clutter, or more precisely, the lack of it. Like a vacuum, Grenney rids rooms of the superfluous. His preferred color palette of chalky hues is a far cry from the vivid lacquered yellow of Nancy Lancaster. His work is cool and collected. "Everything I do is very considered but still looks casual," Grenney says. "Supreme elegance starts with comfort—the most important thing of all."

An admirer of David Hicks, for whom he worked long ago, Grenney follows in his footsteps not only with his edited approach to decorating, but also in his very home. For the past thirty years, Grenney has been the proud owner of the Temple, the eighteenth-century Palladian folly in Suffolk that Hicks restored in the 1950s.

Opposite A former director of the most old guard of English firms, Colefax & Fowler, Veere Grenney has evolved a much more relaxed and casual style. **Below** Like his former employer David Hicks, Grenney combines traditional furnishings with modern, but often mellows them out with palliative colors. **Overleaf** At the Temple, his Palladian folly in Suffolk, Grenney created the drawing room atmosphere almost entirely with paint, his signature shade of Temple Pink.

50 | Kit Kemp

1956–

"Be as bold as you dare."

Kit Kemp came to decorating in a roundabout way. Wishing to see more of her workaholic husband, she joined him as co-owner of the couple's Firmdale Hotels group, in the role of design director. Responsible for the look of a string of boutique hotels in London and New York, **the self-taught Kemp has made her eclectic, patchwork, fashion-driven style a global phenomenon, changing the face of hip hotels from exercises in black to colorful playgrounds.**

Kemp believes in "a sense of arrival and an adventure throughout the building." Audacious color combinations define Kemp's work. So, too, does an artisanal touch, with hand-embroidered textiles covering mile-high headboards and traditional crafts hanging from walls, as at the recently opened Whitby Hotel in Manhattan, where a modern bar sits beneath masses of traditional baskets handmade in England. Combining English freedom with "the freshness of American interiors," Kemp has earned legions of fans on both sides of the pond, with her Ham Yard Hotel in London and the Crosby Street Hotel in New York proving particularly successful.

Kemp recently turned down an offer to design the home of Tesla entrepreneur Elon Musk, preferring her hotels. Her influence on residential design has nonetheless been huge; her hotels are popular with interior design professionals, and they never fail to inspire individuality, quirkiness, and bright colors—lots of them—when the guest goes home. With fabric collections and a furniture line for the alternative fashion retailer Anthropologie, the Kit Kemp look continues to make its way into the home.

Above Known for her bold color sense, Kit Kemp strives for her design work to "feel carefree—and you can't do that without color." **Opposite** Dramatically tall headboards, covered in artistic fabrics, are a signature of Kemp's work; the one seen here is located in a suite at Firmdale's Soho Hotel in London. **Overleaf** Kemp exported her exuberant style to Rossferry, her house in Barbados, where her choice of vivid colors seems made for the Caribbean locale.

51 | Ben Pentreath
1971–

> "The most magical—and, of course, elusive—constituent of English decoration is gentle, slow-roasted time."

Architect-designer **Ben Pentreath has the highest profile of England's new generation of taste-makers**, due largely to the patronage of the Prince of Wales. A classicist, Pentreath designs august facades almost certain to earn historic status someday. But in his interiors, he is much less reverential, practicing his very English brand of eclecticism.

His great talent is respecting traditional decoration and furniture while knowing just when to take liberties with them. When the situation calls for restraint, as when he's working for the Duke and Duchess of Cambridge, Pentreath can do a room bearing the hallmarks of classic English tailoring. Yet to a roomful of brown furniture, Pentreath will frequently introduce some mid-century modern chairs or shot-in-the-arm colors, giving it a twenty-first-century freedom.

A cheerleader for English style, Pentreath has used social media brilliantly to advance his philosophy as well as his work and that of his peers—and sometimes that of David Hicks, whom Pentreath reveres. International fans of his Instagram feed and his widely read blog know every cushion in his Bloomsbury flat and every plate in the Welsh dresser of his Dorset house, the Old Parsonage. Adding to his accomplishments are two splendid books and a Bloomsbury retail shop, Pentreath and Hall, championing the quirky charms of the English point of view.

Left Ben Pentreath's updated approach to traditional English decorating and his command of social media have given him the highest profile of England's young designers. **Opposite** Pentreath's London flat, with its Hans Wegner chair and Fornasetti cabinet, is well known to his many admirers from Instagram. **Overleaf** Bold fabrics and punched-up colors, mixed with classic but unfashionable brown furniture, are the foundation of Pentreath's design work.

THE GLOBALISTS

STÉPHANE BOUDIN

GEORGES GEFFROY

HENRI SAMUEL

VALERIAN STUX RYBAR

FRANÇOIS CATROUX

ALBERTO PINTO

CHRISTIAN LIAIGRE

JACQUES GRANGE

AXEL VERVOORDT

THIERRY W. DESPONT

52 Stéphane Boudin

1888–1967

"Nice houses are never finished."

Maison Jansen in Paris was the world's most famous interiors firm for most of the twentieth century, due in no small part to its designer-president, Stéphane Boudin, whose savoir faire drew aristocrats, nabobs, and even Nancy Lancaster, who engaged him to decorate a few rooms at Ditchley Park in Oxfordshire long before she herself wore the Colefax & Fowler mantle.

His interiors bore the hallmarks of traditional French style, which—it's easy to forget now—was considered the essence of sophisticated living for most of the twentieth century. Antique fauteuils, boiserie, and bureau plats were constants in Boudin's work, although meticulously crafted reproductions, produced by Jansen's famed atelier, were also used.

It wasn't all correct good taste. The designer's work could occasionally be flamboyant, as in the London house of the American expat Henry "Chips" Channon and his Guinness-heiress wife. There, in the 1930s, the designer crafted a dining room inspired by the Hall of Mirrors at the Amalienburg in Munich. A Rococo set piece of aquamarine walls and silver-leafed plasterwork, it was reported to have impressed Queen Mary, and is a highlight of twentieth-century interior design.

Other clients included the Duke and Duchess of Windsor—it was said that the designer referred to Wallis as "my Duchess"—the American socialite and Francophile Jayne Wrightsman, and the young Jacqueline Kennedy, who as First Lady insisted the Frenchman decorate the White House, a decision so controversial that American decorators were added to the mix to provide cover.

Left The most elite designer of his day, Stéphane Boudin had a roster of clients that read like an international *Who's Who*. Opposite Socialite and Francophile Jayne Wrightsman, seen here in 1959 in her Maison Jansen–designed Palm Beach library, introduced Boudin to Jacqueline Kennedy, thus paving the way for his decoration of the Kennedy White House. Overleaf Boudin was a natural choice to decorate the Paris house of the Duke and Duchess of Windsor, who engaged a number of fashionable designers throughout their lives.

53 | Georges Geffroy
1903–1971

Achieving prominence in the aftermath of the Second World War, French designer Georges Geffroy was at the heart of that postwar European social swirl, café society. In high demand, Geffroy rekindled interest in French historical styles, rejuvenating them with modern flourishes and helping postwar France to regain its style supremacy.

His clients included the Duff Coopers (for whom Geffroy, working with Charles de Beistegui and architect-designer Emilio Terry, designed the library at the British Embassy in Paris), the tin-mining heir Arturo Lopez-Willshaw, and the socialites Gloria Guinness and Daisy Fellowes. And for them, only the best would do, especially if it was produced in France. Silks from Prelle, velvets from Le Manach (animal prints, in particular), and important antique furniture crafted by the great eighteenth-century

ébénistes shaped the exalted atmosphere of a Geffroy room. But his forte was his lavish use of fabric, which framed not only windows but also doors, stair railings, and, in Gloria Guinness's Paris home, bookshelves and a fireplace mantel. **Paralleling the couturier Christian Dior, another Geffroy client, and his fabric-rich New Look, Geffroy created sumptuous interiors as an escape from the war-ration mentality of the previous decade.**

Serious about his aestheticism in a way rarely seen today, Geffroy did not suffer fools lightly. Once, when arguing the merits of eighteenth-century French architects with Emilio Terry, the two men became so incensed, one hit the other with an umbrella. Baron Alexis de Redé, a Geffroy client who witnessed the exchange, noted, "It was a period when people felt passionately about things."

Left Animal-print fabrics, specifically tiger- or panther-patterned silk velvet from Le Manach, were fixtures in much of Geffroy's work, including this library he designed for the Paris home of Antenor Patiño in the late 1960s. **Opposite** Couturier Christian Dior sought Geffroy's design expertise for his Paris *hôtel particulier*, which was lavished with silks and velvets.

Above Remarking on Geffroy's attention to detail, friend and
client Baron Alexis de Redé said, "If a cushion were in the wrong
place, he would move it." Right A grand Paris salon designed by
Geffroy for Guillaume and Dale de Bonchamps.

54 | Henri Samuel
1904–1996

"My work probably does carry a stamp but it's quite unwilling. And I couldn't describe it."

With a design background that began in 1925 at Maison Jansen under the tutelage of Stéphane Boudin, Henri Samuel became a decorator of choice for the crème of postwar French society, known for lush, historical interiors that were discerning on the one hand, yet surprisingly comfortable on the other.

Samuel's expertise was the more esoteric styles of nineteenth-century France. Decorating for the Count and Countess d'Ornano, he explored Napoleon III, as he did for Guy and Marie-Hélène de Rothschild at their Château de Ferrières. He managed to avoid the stiffness of historical settings by including non-period furnishings, which gave his interiors a lighter touch. The notable exception was his work assembling eighteenth-century French rooms at the Metropolitan Museum of Art's Wrightsman Galleries.

As mindful of history as he was, Samuel possessed a modern streak, which blossomed in his own *hôtel particulier* on rue du Faubourg Saint-Honoré in Paris. The designer broke ground there by placing contemporary art and furniture, such as a Plexiglas-and-brass chair by artist Philippe Hiquily, in close proximity to French Empire pieces. The effect was so shocking to early 1970s France and, subsequently, so influential **Samuel blurred the rigid boundaries that once governed French decorating.** For his protégé, the esteemed designer Jacques Grange, Samuel's open-minded approach to decorating was liberating: "I learnt, by working with him, the art of jumping with a great freedom from classicism to modernity."

Above left By the time he opened his own firm at the age of sixty-six, Henri Samuel had amassed a loyal clientele, garnered from his days as director of Alavoine et Cie, one of France's premier decorating concerns. **Left** Samuel's Paris home rocked the world of French decorating with its daring mix of traditional furnishings and adventurous contemporary furniture. **Opposite** One of Samuel's most noted projects was the Paris apartment he designed in the 1970s for Count and Countess Hubert d'Ornano, whose grand salon was richly appointed in nineteenth-century style. **Overleaf** The "winter garden" of the Gutfreund residence in New York City might be the most photographed of Samuel's work in America.

55 | Valerian Stux Rybar
1919–1990

> "I think we are all tired of white walls and oversize pieces of art stranded in bare rooms."

He was born in Yugoslavia and based in Manhattan, and he never met a surface he wasn't prepared to mirror. Valerian Stux Rybar was a rarity in late twentieth-century decorating: an American designer who possessed an utterly European point of view. **At a time when most designers were paring down their work and going casual, Rybar did the opposite, lavishing his interiors with a worldly luxury and a whiff of decadence and royal entitlement that suggested Gstaad and Monte Carlo.**

For a glittering clientele whose last names included Onassis, Niarchos, and Rothschild, Rybar decorated to the hilt, even their parties, seemingly never limited by budget. Like a couturier, Rybar enlisted craftsmen to customize interiors that were so detailed and elaborate he became known as the world's most expensive decorator. Pricing was positioning for him. Bespoke finishes, embellished surfaces, and extravagant fabrics expressed a distinctly European idea of grandeur. In one client's bathroom, he installed mother-of-pearl panels. For another, he used satin embellished with gold thread—literally cloth of gold. Yet for all their opulence, his interiors were remarkably pragmatic. "The real luxury today is not that one incredible piece of furniture," said Rybar. "It's perfect cooking and grooming facilities and perfect storage."

In the seventies, a new layer was added to his work, and it suited him well: the hedonism of the decade. Look no farther than Rybar's own Manhattan bathroom, where he mirrored the walls and ceiling—he really did have a thing for mirror—and installed a brushed stainless steel bathtub and a provocative display of wooden heads wearing leather masks.

Above left Born in Yugoslavia, Valerian Rybar never abandoned his European point of view even after moving to America.
Left Rybar's Manhattan living room reflected the sexy seventies, especially his use of coral velvet and stainless steel accents.
Opposite In socialite Sao Schlumberger's Paris residence, Rybar rebuilt the library with tortoiseshell-veneered, stainless steel–trimmed bookcases and a steel-plated floor. **Overleaf** The extravagant use of mirror defined Rybar's career, never more so than in the Paris residence of his partner, designer Jean-François Daigre.

56 | François Catroux
1936–

"Coming to me is a bit like going to Cartier.
I have things made to order."

Entrenched in the worlds of decorating and fashion—his wife, Betty, was a muse to Yves Saint Laurent—the Algerian-born designer François Catroux made one of the splashiest debuts ever when he decorated fashion designer Mila Schön's Milan showroom in 1967. So much publicity surrounded his first project Catroux shot to the top of his profession like a rocket, quickly earning him an elite, and international, clientele that most designers spend decades cultivating. Catroux has remained firmly on top ever since.

Although he has been known to tread in traditional territory, more often than not he's firmly in the present, if not the future. Working at first in an ultra-contemporary style heavy on metal and plastic, Catroux eventually settled into a less extreme style that is still modern and refined, not just in his clients' impressive houses, but in their yachts and planes, too. Above all, Catroux values order in his interiors, with an emphasis on architecture. "Masses that melt into space, different qualities of transparency, various levels—that's what I like," he claims. "Nothing must overwhelm the eye."

Now in his eighties, Catroux continues to design interiors that are exciting, modern, and much in demand. **But what's most impressive about Catroux is that even six decades into his career, his work has never lost its coolness factor.** That might explain why the octogenarian is now designing for the children of his longtime clients, including Crown Princess Marie-Chantal of Greece and Andrés and Lauren Santo Domingo.

Left François Catroux has been at the top of his profession for his entire career, six decades and counting. **Opposite** In his Paris apartment, circa 1969, the designer explored the far reaches of modern. **Overleaf** Neutrals—"I don't like primary colors"—describe the bulk of Catroux's work, including the London home of Crown Princess Marie-Chantal of Greece and family.

57 | Alberto Pinto

1943–2012

"I try above all to serve people with considerable obligations. By introducing a little fantasy and good life into their pitiless universe."

Designer to both French heads of state and Middle Eastern royalty, Alberto Pinto was a man of the world—born in Casablanca, based in Paris—**whose cultured point of view produced some of the most internationally flavorful work of any designer living in France.** He himself boiled his style down to this: "A mix of cultures. It really sums me up."

For clients seeking traditional Gallic elegance, Pinto could out-French the French, assembling rooms of velvet-and-ormolu splendor rivaling anything seen in past centuries, though without characteristic French formality; a Pinto interior was neither stiff nor uneasy. Decades into his career, the designer earned the right to say, "I pride myself on knowing how to bring together immensity and comfort." Immensity, indeed. Yet as accomplished as he was in grand manner decorating, Pinto could effortlessly switch gears to interiors that were modern and refreshing or, especially, exotic and Orientalist in tone—a career-long interest that spoke to his Moroccan roots.

With a flair for *l'art de vivre*, Pinto was also a dab hand at *l'art de la table*, which he practiced using his staggering collection of tableware. It included antique embroidered napery, Sèvres and Meissen dinner services, and nineteenth-century crystal. Classic white linen and china were not in his vocabulary. Pinto was so enamored of table settings he became a highly successful designer of china and linens, as renowned for both as he was for interior design.

Left Alberto Pinto was that rare decorator who was skilled in distinctly different styles, including French traditionalism and Orientalism. **Opposite** The designer's own dining room in Paris, with its velvet-cloaked walls and niches, was a seminal moment in late twentieth-century grand-manner decorating. **Overleaf** Comfort was never overlooked in Pinto's work, even when a room's atmosphere was as majestic as this Paris residence.

THE SPLENDOR OF FRANCE

61 | Thierry W. Despont

1948–

"I do not design shelter."

The French architect-interior designer Thierry W. Despont does things big. Big, as in the restoration of the Statue of Liberty, the Ritz Paris, and the Cartier Fifth Avenue flagship as well as the Carlyle Hotel in Manhattan. **Don't bother calling him to design your home unless you're a leader of industry, fashion, or society.** His exalted clientele includes Jayne Wrightsman, the Oscar de la Rentas, Bill Gates, and Calvin Klein (who, you almost certainly will have noticed, appears as a key client in multiple profiles in this book).

Wielding absolute control over his residential work, Despont addresses architecture, interiors, and landscaping in an all-encompassing approach, researched and executed to the highest standard, whatever the style. He once explained, "I like to create a small universe. From the master plan to the doorknobs, from the trees planted outside to the way people will sit and eat and dance inside, you create and control a whole microcosm."

His projects include a 20,000-square-foot house for Gates and the Montauk estate once owned by Andy Warhol, all so fine-tuned he consistently wins the highest praise from the most demanding of clients, among them the retail impresario Mickey Drexler, of Gap and J. Crew, who proclaimed, "Thierry is as good as it gets."

***

Opposite Although his clients pay dearly for his services, Despont says the houses he designs "are not investments. They are investments in joie de vivre." **Below** Despont is known for executing projects on a big scale, like this house in Aspen, Colorado.

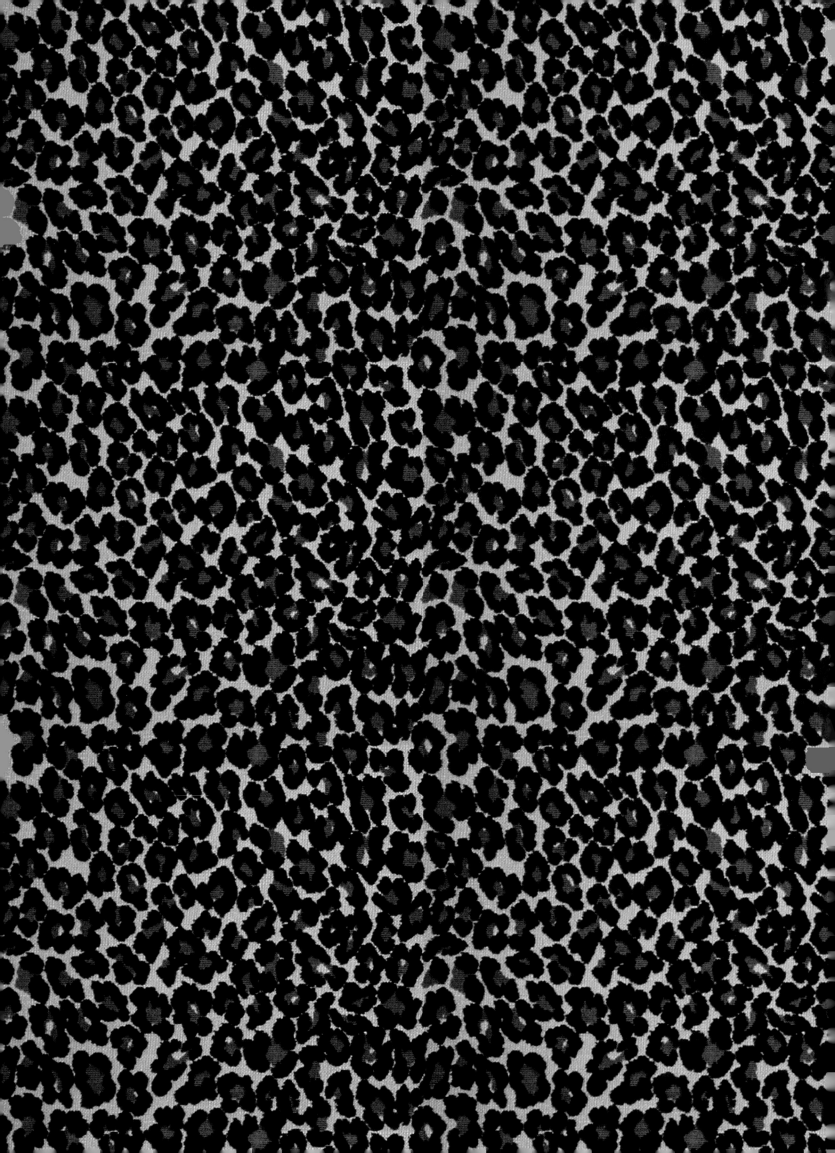

THE GRANDEES

RENZO
MONGIARDINO

DENNING AND
FOURCADE

MAC II

IRVINE &
FLEMING

MARIO BUATTA

DAVID EASTON

MARK HAMPTON

PETER MARINO

62 | Renzo Mongiardino
1916–1998

"The contemporary is really not in my nature."

Admirers often referred to him as a wizard. Walls inlaid with marquetry skyscrapers, a living room fashioned into a Bedouin tent—these were not fantasies. They were realities for Renzo Mongiardino, one of the design world's most inventive, and enigmatic, figures.

Mongiardino, who was based in Milan, was skilled at identifying a room's architectural strengths and weaknesses. But once his analysis was complete, the designer switched gears completely and dramatically, conceiving wildly imaginative solutions to the architecture. Under Mongiardino's spell, walls were treated to murals, marbleized finishes, imitation leather, textiles, and trims made to look like paneling, while ceilings were magnificently "coffered" with trompe l'oeil paintwork. Often the effect was theatrical—Mongiardino was, after all, a sometime set designer—but it somehow never strayed into gimmickry. Always exquisitely researched and rendered, his decorative illusions were only for a rarefied clientele so rich it was once described as a "kidnapper's wish list."

But it was Mongiardino's unique and total way of channeling the romantic past that was his great achievement. Whether the mood was Near East exoticism, as in Lee Radziwill's London drawing room, immortalized in a famous Cecil Beaton photograph, or the faded grandeur of Lampedusa's *The Leopard*, Mongiardino had a gift for referencing the past without getting stuck in it, something that his patron Marella Agnelli admired: "His nostalgia for the past . . . never prevented him from conjuring interiors that had a timeless quality about them."

Opposite Once describing his design philosophy, Mongiardino quoted the ancient Greek philosopher Zeno, who remarked upon seeing the then newly built Parthenon, "Absolutely beautiful. It looks as though it has always been there!" **Left** Although it looks centuries old, the ceiling mural of this library, in a restored Roman palazzo, was the creation of Mongiardino and his craftsmen. **Overleaf** Mongiardino's imagination ran rampant in this nineteenth-century villa in Bologna, Italy, where an enchanting trompe l'oeil garden was painted on the living room ceiling.

63 | Denning and Fourcade

ROBERT DENNING 1927–2005
VINCENT FOURCADE 1934–1992

"Outrageous luxury is what our clients want.
We have taught them to prefer excess."

The design world's oddest couple, Vincent Fourcade and Robert Denning were an unlikely partnership from the start: the former grew up privileged in France; the latter less so, in the Bronx; and together they lacked any formal design training. Nevertheless, **they conquered Manhattan spectacularly with an opulent style that dazzled the richest and the mightiest of the 1980s.**

"We were about ways to show money," Fourcade admitted, offering a forthright explanation for a shameless excess that seemed perfectly normal then but might seem tone-deaf today. A modern adaptation of Victorian and Edwardian styles, the Denning and Fourcade look required a lot of fabric, a lot of custom passementerie that often cost as much as the sofa or chair, and a lot of funds. Damask, brocade, ormolu, bronze, vermeil, and marble prevailed. You could be smothered in the cushions of one of their down sofas. Among their signatures were the double-sided sofa and those *fin de siècle* throwbacks, Austrian shades. "The upholsterer is the five-and-ten," Denning once said. "A chair costs five thousand. A sofa costs ten." Please adjust for inflation.

It was easy to mock their sumptuous and even suffocating style, but it took extraordinary skill to execute, and exceptional sophistication to appreciate. The partners' work enticed such boldfaced names as Jayne Wrightsman, Henry Kissinger, and Oscar de la Renta. But without a doubt, their most high-profile effort was for the financier Henry Kravis and Carolyne Roehm, who at that time was a fashion designer, having once worked for Oscar de la Renta. When their dining room appeared on the cover of the *New York Times Magazine*, it prompted such a backlash that both the decorators and their clients became unfortunate symbols of everything wrong with the 1980s. But take a step back, and the decorating is extraordinary. We'll probably never see the likes of it again.

Left Whether decorating for themselves, such as the living room of their Paris apartment, seen here, or for clients, Denning and Fourcade aimed for "something totally removed from the complications of the day." **Opposite** In client Oscar de la Renta's Manhattan apartment, their signature piece, a triumph of fabric, passementerie, and the upholsterer's art: a custom double-sided sofa. **Overleaf** Denning and Fourcade, photographed among the splendor of their New York City townhouse in the late 1970s, insisted that their rooms looked as though they were "never touched by a decorator." They were probably alone in that assessment.

MAC II

MICA ERTEGUN 1927–
CHESSY RAYNER 1931–1998

"Too many objects confuse the eye."

"It sounds more like a trucking firm," cofounder Mica Ertegun has often quipped about the name of her firm, MAC II. But Ertegun and her partner, the late Chessy Rayner, were two of the most glamorous designers of their day. Rayner was a Pond's cold cream heiress. Ertegun, who as a young woman fled her native Romania with the royal family, was married to the founder of Atlantic Records and ran with Mick Jagger. MAC II—short for "Mica and Chessy"—overcame early accusations of dilettantism with a style that was highly edited and discriminating, and could only have grown from the designers' own lives spent in the world's finest houses. Their uniform of Madame Grès jersey dresses and turbans only added to the allure.

After an early flirtation with sixties-era psychedelic prints, Rayner and Ertegun found their direction in their own personal style. MAC II rooms were as disciplined, restrained, and formidable as its principals were walking the red carpet into a black-tie benefit at the Park Avenue Armory. Their muted backgrounds—a buffed-out palette and pale, solid-colored upholstery—served primarily to highlight the art and antiques collections that their lofty clientele usually brought with them.

Bill Blass described his own Manhattan apartment by Rayner and Ertegun as "very spare settings for very good things," but he could have been describing MAC II's entire body of work. **The spare chic of Blass's neoclassical apartment reflected the rare, perfect match of client and designer.** With its ivory walls, French-polished mahogany, and highly regarded Grand Tour collections, the apartment is arguably the most successful traditional scheme of the late twentieth century, and certain to be admired by generations to come.

Opposite Mica Ertegun (right) and Chessy Rayner were known to dress much like their interiors, in neutrals. "Color I like in carpets and paintings," said Ertegun. **Below** The partners' greatest work was for Bill Blass, whose spare but impeccably appointed Sutton Place penthouse apartment, seen here, ranks as one of the legendary interiors of the twentieth century.

65 Irvine & Fleming

KEITH IRVINE 1928–2011
THOMAS FLEMING 1933–

"It mustn't show like you've made the effort.
It mustn't show like you've spent the money."

"Comfortable seating groups, black lacquer, busts, Staffordshire figures, well-worn carpets, and always books." Although Keith Irvine was naming his favorite design elements, his list could just as easily describe the work of his firm, Irvine & Fleming, an exponent of aristocratic English coziness.

Born in Scotland, Irvine began his career assisting the great John Fowler, remembering mostly that he bore the brunt of Fowler's snobbishness in the houses of earls and marquesses. Moving to America, he had a brief and tortuous spell working for Sister Parish before venturing out on his own. He cofounded Clarence House fabrics in 1961, then went on to build a thriving interior design practice that employed a number of soon-to-be famous designers, including Mario Buatta, who assisted Irvine in the 1960s, and Thomas Fleming, who became his business partner in 1967.

Of all the American practitioners of English style, Irvine & Fleming was the truest to the original. Their rooms were expensively and exquisitely detailed, but they also always had loose, comfortable floor plans, flashes of wit, and a human touch that decorators often strive to edit out. They would design the grandest curtains for the grandest room, as perfectly proportioned as John Fowler's, then find a way to "knock down" the room, as the English would say. Believing that "in decorating, the worst sin of all is taking it far too seriously," Irvine and Fleming used their light touch to create the appearance of rooms culled over time—a subtle, sophisticated approach in a country not yet accustomed to the undecorated look.

Irvine never wavered from his English design roots, not even in the 1980s, when other designers' misguided efforts caused him to lament, "There's no more dignity left in ribbons or buttons or bows." Irvine and Fleming continued to do a brisk business with many of America's leading families, including a Kennedy, until their firm's dissolution in 2007.

Left Thomas Fleming believed "Nothing should be too ordered."
Opposite Keith Irvine photographed in the ballroom addition of his much-loved nineteenth-century farm house in New York.
Overleaf Irvine considered this Manhattan apartment as some of their very best work. Ironically, the apartment once belonged to Sister Parish.

66 | Mario Buatta
1935–

"I'm not afraid of having a pink hall because I'm a man."

Opposite A lifelong arch-traditionalist, Buatta stuck to his guns even during the pared-down nineties: "The shell of a minimalist room gets shoddy very quickly." **Above** It was this fabric-rich bedroom for the 1984 Kips Bay Show House, at the peak of the 1980s English country craze, that earned Mario Buatta the nickname the Prince of Chintz. **Overleaf** Everything Buatta holds dear can be found in his much-photographed Upper East Side living room: chintz, blue-and-white porcelain, and dog portraits festooned with bows and ribbon.

A friendship with Rose Cumming, an early job working for designer Keith Irvine, and annual visits with his idol, John Fowler, were a few early hints at the remarkable career to come for Mario Buatta. The best-known of the elite New York decorators, the affable, publicity-savvy, very social Buatta spent years turning up the volume of the English country house style for American eyes until it became the must-have look of the 1980s.

Buatta grew up unimpressed with the white Deco-style interiors of his childhood home on Staten Island. Instead he gravitated to the traditional, WASP-y homes of his friends, which educated him in the importance of a house looking lived-in. But it was the work of Fowler and Nancy Lancaster, specifically photos of Lancaster's butter-yellow drawing room, that gave him a lifelong case of Anglophilia. Lively color palettes (much more saturated than those of his Colefax & Fowler predecessors), English antiques, and dog portraits, sometimes hung from exaggerated ribbons and bows, conjured up an atmosphere of Mayfair in America, nowhere more so than in his own apartment, possibly the most photographed ever.

But Buatta will forever be synonymous with chintz—glazed and unglazed, shirred and ruched, madly colored floral chintz, yard after yard after yard of it used on upholstery and ball-gown curtains. He has used it enthusiastically throughout his career, earning him the nickname the Prince of Chintz, a magazine cover on which he wore a custom chintz suit, and even his own Absolut Vodka advertisement.

The Buatta frenzy reached its peak with his outrageously frothy blue-and-lavender bedroom for the Kips Bay Show House in 1984. The design pendulum would inevitably swing in the opposite direction ten years later, but Buatta remained true to the style he loves, and continues to create English-style interiors for a loyal clientele. Today, a new generation of Americans has come to appreciate Buatta's cheerful, traditional look, thanks to his work on a Charleston house featured regularly in the Bravo reality show *Southern Charm*.

67 | David Easton
1937–

"You really can't have a beautiful room unless you start with a beautiful space."

An architecture degree and an early stint working for mid-century modernism's leading figure, the furniture designer Edward Wormley, might have given David Easton a thoroughly modernist foundation, but it was a subsequent employer, Parish-Hadley Associates, that led him to become one of America's most accomplished traditional decorators. Recalling his time spent toiling alongside Sister Parish and Albert Hadley until striking out on his own, Easton says, "The education I received was invaluable."

Although he burst on the scene during the 1980s at the peak of the mania for the English country house style, Easton really produces work that draws from the neoclassical well, whether it is traditional or—more often than people realize—contemporary. Order and correctness define an Easton interior, as do architectural underpinnings, which come at a cost. His clientele flush with cash, Easton spent the 1980s living out a designer's dream, shopping overseas for $150,000 rugs and $80,000 Regency library tables, all earmarked for multimillion-dollar projects. "I am amazed people have the money to spend on these projects," Easton once said. "Of course, it's great for us that they do."

Of all his rich clients, Easton will forever be associated with one of the eighties' richest: media billionaire John Kluge, and his wife, Patricia. The Kluges, whose favorite pastime was coach driving, engaged Easton to design a Georgian stately in the horse country of Virginia. Albemarle House took on epic proportions, with a splendidly detailed forty-five-room brick house, a chapel, and a museum for their antique carriages, all chronicled in the pages of *Vogue* as the stock market boiled over. It was a moment. But while it might have come to represent that era's grandiosity, it was saved by the flawless elegance and historicism of Easton's execution.

Left David Easton's body of work exhibits three distinct influences: neoclassicism, the English Country House style, and modernism. **Opposite** Easton's most high-profile project was Albemarle, a Virginia estate for the John Kluges built from the ground up; his taste for classicism is evident in its drawing room. **Overleaf** Easton's former weekend retreat, Balderbrae, in Suffern, New York, was a made-for-America version of a traditional English country house.

68 | Mark Hampton
1940–1998

"Minimalism is for the very young."

A gifted decorator, watercolorist, historian, and writer, Mark Hampton might have been America's most well-rounded designer. Although he died twenty years ago, his presence is still felt in the design profession, in his classic primer *Mark Hampton on Decorating*, in his legacy of iconic rooms, and in the design firm that his daughter, Alexa, has successfully continued.

An Indiana native who worked for David Hicks, Parish-Hadley, and McMillen before going solo, Hampton became a sensation thanks to his immense talent and taste, but also his Renaissance-Man charm. Never one to make a statement with a room, he was the perfect society decorator, advocating classicism and tradition. It was a well-mannered, nothing-to-prove approach that seemed a breath of fresh air after the trendiness of the 1970s. But timing, too, played a role. Hampton was in the right place at the right time: eighties-era Manhattan, flush with newly minted Wall Street tycoons and their social aspirations. Already a darling of the establishment—Hampton considered the library he created for the Vanderbilt heir Carter Burden his masterpiece—he soon became highly sought-after by the new guard, who hoped Hampton's patrician style might help smooth their way on Park Avenue.

Prominent himself on the Manhattan social scene, he sat at the best tables with his wife, Duane, and counted Estée Lauder, Brooke Astor, and President George H. W. Bush among his clients. In one of the more high-profile decorating assignments of the 1980s—the overhaul of Blair House, the presidential guesthouse—he collaborated with fellow designer Mario Buatta. Buatta was bold and sometimes outrageous; Hampton was always quiet and correct. "Mark and Mario"—a phrase often heard in decorating circles during the eighties—were like Coke and Pepsi. They competed head-on to be the top dog of Park Avenue, and at times it even approached a good-natured feud, but neither could ever win—they were just different tastes for different people.

Opposite Putting his profession in perspective, Mark Hampton once said, "Decorating is not brain surgery—it's supposed to be fun." **Left** Hampton's best-loved room was arguably his own Upper East Side living room, which evolved with him for decades; in the 1980s, it charmed admirers with its yards of chintz and Edwardian comfort. **Overleaf** The masterpiece of Hampton's career was Carter and Susan Burden's New York City library, with its mahogany bookshelves, red wool-damask walls, and dazzling oval desk.

69 | Peter Marino
1949–

"A palace should look like a palace, a loft should look like a loft, and a hot dog stand should look like a hot dog stand."

He is best known for a sartorial about-face that made jaws drop. One day he was wearing natty bow ties. The next, in late middle age, it was a biker-gang uniform of black leather, bare arms, and skull rings, and it has been that ever since. Peter Marino's career never skipped a beat through it all, though, producing work of such high caliber he would be at the top of the list for any client, at least for those who can afford him.

After passing through Andy Warhol's Factory, Marino received three early commissions that set his career off and running: the Manhattan homes of Warhol, Yves Saint Laurent and Pierre Bergé, and Gianni and Marella Agnelli. With that, any interior designer would have been on his way. But Marino delivered, decade after decade, and without anybody ever pigeonholing him. **Marino's greatest distinction is that he's not identified with any one style, only that he can work in any style at the highest level that the decorating world can demand.** Whether traditional or the extreme edge of modern, every Marino interior is the epitome of luxury, with complex finishes, custom-designed fabrics, and highly specialized craftsmanship.

"The triple play of art, architecture, and fashion is what most excites me," said Marino. "I have my finger in all three pies." Indeed, in recent years it has been his association with the fashion industry that has earned him international stardom, not to mention front-row seats at the Paris collections. As the designated architect for the likes of Chanel, Dior, and Louis Vuitton, Marino has created some of the most visually exciting boutiques in the world and established design as a key branding component in fashion.

Opposite It may be hard to believe, but the Peter Marino whose uniform is now black leather was once known for bespoke suits and bow ties. **Below** Entrenched in the fashion world, Marino was responsible for making Giancarlo Giammetti's apartment the talk of Paris.

LIKE
NO OTHER

DONALD DESKEY

WILLIAM HAINES

TONY DUQUETTE

JOHN DICKINSON

ARTHUR ELROD

BILL WILLIS

CARLETON VARNEY

JOHN SALADINO

JOSEPH D'URSO

ROSE TARLOW

70 Donald Deskey
1894–1989

"[I have] never done a period design and never will."

The 1925 Exposition Internationale des Arts Décoratifs et Industriels Modernes—the pioneering decorative arts exhibition held in Paris—formally introduced the Art Deco style to the public and created a sensation. A young artist, Donald Deskey, was so electrified by what he saw there he returned home to America and became one of this country's leading proponents of the new style.

Donald Deskey set the course of Art Deco in the United States. His interpretation of it was less ornamental and luxurious than its French counterpart and distinctly American, reflecting the Machine Age and the gleaming Manhattan skyscrapers sprouting up around him. Sleek furniture, inventive finishes, and the use of new materials like aluminum, nickel, Bakelite, cork, and patent leather made Deskey's work thrilling to style setters Abby Aldrich Rockefeller and Helena Rubinstein, who engaged him to decorate their homes in his radical style.

His masterpiece, largely intact today, was the interior of New York's best-loved example of Art Deco: Radio City Music Hall, a 6,015-seat theater in Rockefeller Center where, in 1932, Deskey directed the work on every detail, from vast murals down to the carpeting and ash stands. Every bit as impressive as its vast foyer and hall are the nooks and crannies, including the Nicotine Room, a men's smoking room where Deskey treated the walls to simulate embossed cigarette foil, and a women's lounge enveloped in a mural documenting the history of cosmetics. For glamour, it simply cannot be beaten.

Deskey later applied his innovative thinking to industrial design, becoming one of its most successful practitioners. Although most of us are unaware of it, the packaging and logos of many of America's best-known household products can be traced back to him, including Jif peanut butter and Crest toothpaste.

Above left Before he became an industrial designer, Donald Deskey was behind some of New York City's most glamorous Art Deco interiors. **Left** For Samuel "Roxy" Rothafel, the man responsible for opening Radio City Music Hall, Deskey designed this apartment, the so-called Roxy Suite at the theater. His private quarters, including its cherrywood-paneled living room, are still intact.
Opposite Deskey created his Man's [Smoking] Room, with striped cork walls, for an exhibition at the American Designers' Gallery, New York City, in 1928.

71 | William Haines

1900–1973

"I've never been quite divorced from show business.
I'm still an actor who's hanging some curtains."

Above William Haines, circa 1930, during his movie star days.
Opposite The epitome of mid-century glamour: socialite Betsy Bloomingdale, standing by the fireplace in her Haines-decorated living room, at a Little Black Tie Dinner she hosted in 1959.
Overleaf Haines's signature low hostess chairs—designed to exaggerate women's legs and show off their dresses—were fixtures in most of his rooms, including the living room at Sunnylands.

They say there are no second acts in show business, but William "Billy" Haines, a successful film star who turned to decorating during the 1930s, proved that adage wrong. Trading on his good taste and his Hollywood contacts, **Haines became the first Southern California power decorator, inventing a glamorous new look, rooted in casual Los Angeles living, that elevated the homes of the movie industry.**

At the beginning of his career, Haines married patrician decor with Hollywood spectacle. English antiques and eighteenth-century wallpaper provided the pedigree, while lavish trims, stylized murals, and Chinoiserie decorations—a hallmark of Haines's work throughout his career—provided the drama. But as forties-era modernism swept the West Coast, Haines pivoted his look, adopting a streamlined sensibility that came to be synonymous with the California good life. It was a look that was uniquely his. Unusually low sofas and chairs, designed by Haines to show off dresses and long legs, promoted easy cocktail banter. Luxurious European traditions like trapunto (fabric quilting) and embroidery were tempered with colors and natural materials reflecting the landscape of the Golden State. Less theatrical than his early work, this easygoing modernism propelled Haines's career and attracted a social clientele, including Betsy Bloomingdale and the Annenbergs, whose meticulously preserved Rancho Mirage estate, Sunnylands, is considered one of Haines's greatest projects.

Despite his success, Haines rarely decorated beyond the West Coast, the notable exception being the American Embassy in London, for Ambassador Walter Annenberg, at the end of his career. But it was this distance from the East Coast design establishment that gave Haines the freedom to pursue a style all his own. Even today, decades after the designer's death, the Billy Haines look is unmistakable and remains the essence of Southern California style.

72 | Tony Duquette
1914–1999

"Scavenging is my passion, instead of drinking or gambling."

No other designer could make a silk purse out of a sow's ear quite like Tony Duquette, the wizard of Los Angeles, whose work beguiled even the most discerning individuals, including Elsie de Wolfe. **Duquette's genius was his ability to transform the mundane into the extraordinary, showing the same enthusiasm for dimestore treasures as he did luxurious materials.** "I work equally with burlap and velvet," he once said. Rubber sandals, metal vegetable steamers, and lemon juicers were fashioned into interior embellishments so marvelous they have since become design legend.

A Duquette interior—notably his Beverly Hills house, Dawnridge, where his longtime collaborator and business partner Hutton Wilkinson still works—was a world of fantasy and exoticism. He had a fondness for malachite, both genuine and imitation, and for extravagant patterns, especially leopard-print carpets and fabrics. Coral branches, too—but were they real, or were they fake?—were constants in his work.

Movie set decoration was a natural for Duquette's make-believe style. For forties- and fifties-era MGM musicals such as *The Ziegfeld Follies* and *Kismet*, the designer created unforgettable backdrops that were larger than life. Always creating something, Duquette even succeeded at designing jewelry, the one area of his work ruled strictly by the authentic. Precious gems were imperative when clients like the Duchess of Windsor were buying.

Opposite Always the showman, Duquette posed onstage in the ballroom of his Los Angeles studio. **Below** The office at Duquette's Beverly Hills home, Dawnridge, loaded with his fantastical creations.

The drawing room of
Dawnridge. Its splendor
is maintained today by
Duquette's protégé and
business partner, Hutton
Wilkinson.

73 | John Dickinson

1920–1982

"Design is like vocabulary. There are so many ways to say the same familiar things, so originality is paramount."

With an independent streak a mile wide, John Dickinson was the antithesis of what was expected of a prominent designer. He preferred living in San Francisco to New York, detested travel, and unashamedly fashioned interiors that reflected him, not his clients. After all, his clients hired him for his look, Dickinson reasoned. Then there was his work, whose peculiarities were so original they earned him a cult following.

Hard to define but always unforgettable, a Dickinson interior ran the gamut from clean and monochromatic to simply unusual, which rightly described his own residence, a former firehouse. Dickinson painted the walls and ceilings to look ancient and crumbling, while he concealed his clothes closet in carved wooden doors that resembled a row of Victorian townhouses. To this, Dickinson added his own **self-styled furniture, which was so lacking in convention, yet so copied, and so expensive today, it might be his greatest legacy.**

"I simply felt there was a need for a new motif in design. It's just a way of making a leg look different," Dickinson explained of his animalistic furniture. Usually made of plaster or wood, these pieces often looked ready to pounce; for example, there was his "Etruscan" series of tables and chairs, with legs mimicking a feline. Another direction was his African-inspired table, a primitive three-legged form made modern in white plaster. And then seemingly out of nowhere came his range of galvanized steel tables, with simulated folds of fabric turning the concept of the skirted table on its head. It all added up to a look that was his and his alone.

Left John Dickinson once conceded that "the way my designs evolved seemed to frighten a lot of people." **Opposite** Dickinson's three-legged African-inspired table, avidly collected today, was among the many furnishings in his San Francisco home that bordered on bizarre.

74 | Arthur Elrod
1924–1974

Palm Springs was the place to be in the Southern California of the 1950s and 1960s. The desert playground of Frank Sinatra and his Rat Pack, it was also home to many important modern architects and designers, notably Arthur Elrod, who became the favorite decorator for the modernist houses designed by esteemed architects Richard Neutra and John Lautner, among others. Elrod also played an off-camera role in the quintessential photograph of that era: Slim Aarons's *Poolside Gossip* (1970), which captured two highly coiffed socialites lounging poolside at the iconic Kaufmann House. Elrod had designed the interiors.

His greatest accomplishment, however, was his own Palm Springs residence, which he designed with Lautner in 1968. Even today **the Elrod House is breathtaking in its radicalness**. Fully integrated into its desert landscape, the five-room house was carved into rock, which serves as interior walls in some rooms. Its most prominent feature is a circular living room capped by a radial, poured-concrete dome spanning sixty feet. Bearing a striking resemblance to a spaceship, the room is surrounded by frameless floor-to-ceiling windows offering a panoramic view of the desert terrain by day and the twinkling lights of Palm Springs at night.

Deemed the ultimate bachelor pad by *Playboy* magazine, the house became associated with that era's other cultural landmark: Sean Connery's star turn as James Bond. It was in the Elrod House's living room where Bambi and Thumper gave Bond a licking in the 1971 film *Diamonds Are Forever*.

Above left During the mid-twentieth century, Arthur Elrod was the decorator behind some of Palm Springs' finest houses, including those of the comedian Bob Hope and the actor Laurence Harvey. **Left** An Elrod interior in Coeur d'Alene, Idaho. **Opposite** With its awe-inspiring radial ceiling, Elrod House in Palm Springs was, according to its owner, "better than living in a piece of sculpture."

75 | Bill Willis
1937–2009

"My discovery of the Islamic world has been an astounding experience."

Above It was said that designer Bill Willis understood Morocco "like no one else." **Opposite** Yves Saint Laurent considered his Willis-designed library at Villa Oasis, his residence in Marrakech, to be his favorite room of all.

Bill Willis might be the most influential designer you've never heard of. An American expat who called Marrakech home, Willis is the man most responsible for the so-called Moroccan look that has been a major design theme over the last few decades.

After time spent in Rome, where he owned an antiques shop and designed accessories for Valentino and bath towels for Yves Saint Laurent, Willis decamped to Marrakech in 1967 with close friends J. Paul Getty Jr. and his wife, Talitha, the most prominent trust-fund bohemians of the sixties. A louche lifestyle fueled by drugs and populated by the beautiful people ensued, but Willis nonetheless managed to decorate both the Gettys' newly acquired residence, an eighteenth-century palace, and his own, a former royal harem. His efforts were so enticingly decadent, and so unlike anything else, Willis quickly became Marrakech's most sought-after decorator for members of the European elite, who were beginning to desire their own Moroccan retreats.

Enamored with the languishing artistic traditions of his adopted country, Willis revived them, seeking out local tradesmen to reproduce centuries-old crafts. Glazed tile, mosaics, brickwork, and wood painted with Islamic motifs played commanding roles in Willis's interiors, as did *tadelakt*, a type of glazed plasterwork that the designer liberated from the hammam, the public bathhouses where it had been used for centuries. It was Willis's fresh approach to Moroccan traditions, which he interpreted—and, in a sense, pared down—using a Western eye, that came to define the country's aesthetic. As client and close friend Pierre Bergé put it, "It was Bill who coined the design vocabulary of today's Morocco."

Appointed to design Marie-Hélène de Rothschild's house in Marrakech as well as a garden pavilion for Marella Agnelli, Willis's influence was felt directly by the ancient city and, by reputation, well beyond. But his most celebrated work was for Bergé and Yves Saint Laurent, who engaged Willis to revive the interiors of the Villa Oasis, the former home of painter Jacques Majorelle, which the couple purchased along with its famous garden. Among his many recherché residences, Saint Laurent counted the villa's Willis-designed library as his "favorite room in the world."

76 | Carleton Varney
1937–

"Does the flower garden exist with only one flower and one or two colors? Absolutely not!"

Design legend Dorothy Draper's greatest cheerleader, Carleton Varney began his career as Draper's protégé, joining her legendary decorating firm in 1960 and taking charge of it after her death. In his book *There's No Place Like Home*, Varney wrote jokingly, "Much to everyone's surprise, I did not push Mrs. Draper down the elevator shaft to become president of this company." Still at the helm of Dorothy Draper & Company decades later, Varney has kept Draper's name and her product designs alive and thriving. But **Varney has managed to become a decorating legend in his own right, famous for bringing unbridled exuberance to his work.**

Trained by Draper in her love of bold colors—"Show me nothing that looks like gravy!" she used to say—Varney took color even further. He is known for saturating interiors with Technicolor shades of red, green, and pink, and then turning up the volume with mad combinations and gutsy patterns. Preppy and old-school, with a penchant for bold chintzes and pairs of Staffordshire dogs, his traditional style was made for Palm Beach, where he refreshed the Colony Hotel, and he would make the history books alone for his psychedelic work at the classic Greenbrier hotel and resort in West Virginia. But it has also earned him a loyal clientele of often big personalities, such as Ethel Merman and Joan Crawford.

Varney is tireless. Over six decades, the former schoolteacher has written many design books and taught the how-tos of decorating in a syndicated newspaper column, "Your Family Decorator." Every bit as savvy as his mentor, Varney today sells his furnishings collection on the Home Shopping Network. Draper would have approved.

Left Varney credits his mentor, Dorothy Draper, for teaching him "how to keep magic alive within the tradition." **Opposite** The designer's high-spirited makeover of the Stoneleigh Hotel in Dallas reflects his lifelong dedication to energizing colors and bold patterns. **Overleaf** Michigan's landmark Grand Hotel on Mackinac Island has relied on Varney to decorate its interiors, like this lobby, since the 1970s.

77 | John Saladino

1939–

"A tweezered, mirrored, gilt, flocked, overstuffed, overcarpeted environment offends me."

"Any work of art must be in constant tension," says the painter-cum-designer John Saladino, whose carefully composed interiors project a range of different personalities, often at the same time. Classical yet modern, mercurial and romantic, Saladino's work is a complexity of moods meant "to create an emotional experience."

"I believe in always bringing something of the ancient world into the twentieth century," he says, summing up the Saladino look as far back as his early days, when he frequently paired modern furniture with antiquities, an unheard-of combination at the time. **His rooms hearken back to Italian precedents, with classical elements such as columns and arches incorporated in the architecture.** His love of "corroded surfaces" led to his development of a scratch-coat plaster treatment for walls that gives his interiors the romance of a crumbling palazzo. Saladino refuses to divulge its formula.

A highly regarded furniture designer, Saladino is best known for his upholstered seating, which is not based on the usual Bridgewater, Lawson, and Tuxedo forms. The backs of his sofas tend to be high, straight, and enveloping, while those of his chairs are so low they barely register. Channel quilting gives them a look all their own. But his greatest creation is surely his trademarked Saladino Lamp, whose tubular glass body topped by a plain paper shade has proven so timeless it prompted fashion designer Michael Kors to call it "the little black dress of lamps."

Left John Saladino broke ground in the seventies by daring to mix antiquities and classical references with unusual modern furniture of his own design. **Opposite** The designer has been known to call his rooms "walk-in paintings," which aptly describes this Santa Barbara, California, interior. **Overleaf** Rough, crumbling-looking plaster walls and distinctive upholstered silhouettes could only be Saladino.

78 Joseph D'Urso
1943–

"I design so that the onus of expression is on the individual, not on a collage of objects."

In the hard-partying Manhattan of the late 1970s, after dinner, after waking from a nap at midnight, the most sophisticated crowd in Manhattan would gather shoulder-to-shoulder on a long leather banquette around a coffee table on wheels in a poetically bare room high in the sky before heading out to Studio 54.

The room would be by Joseph D'Urso, the die-hard minimalist who was one of New York's defining designers during the 1970s and '80s, a disciple of the high-tech look that was the favorite of Manhattan's young style makers. Employing industrial materials, D'Urso's work seemed made for the utilitarian architecture found in that era's other domestic craze: loft living.

In those early days, D'Urso took an unambiguous approach to decorating, seeing interiors in black and white, with glossy white walls that served to "activate the light." Black upholstery, black and stainless steel finishes, and gray-carpeted floors and platforms fleshed out otherwise empty rooms. It all seemed so simple, but a very real talent underpinned it: D'Urso's sensitivity to space and correcting the shortcomings of architecture. The emptiness

was as carefully designed as the furniture. D'Urso often had to defend his extreme minimalism, which had a polarizing effect on people. "The problem is that most people take the term to mean there's nothing there, when in fact the opposite is true," he said.

D'Urso's career has never waned since, although his rooms have grown a little softer. He has had a long association with Knoll; his early pieces are still sought on 1stdibs, his newer designs still in production. But like a singer who had a culture-changing hit early in his career, he will forever be identified with a truly original style that captures a brief magical moment.

Above During the seventies, Joseph D'Urso was New York City's hottest designer and the face of the high-tech look. **Opposite** Whereas D'Urso's earlier work was ultra-minimal and graphic, his more recent interiors, such as this house in the Hamptons, are "more idiomatic." **Overleaf** The apartment that defined 1970s Manhattan: bare glossy walls, leather banquettes, and the mastery of space as only D'Urso could do it, for the fashion designer Calvin Klein.

79 | Rose Tarlow

1946–

"One thing I really do dislike, however, is seeing furniture and interiors that all resemble each other so much that it gets monotonous."

Rose Tarlow, based in Los Angeles, has the career other designers dream of. It began with Melrose House, the antiques shop she transformed into a to-the-trade furniture line considered one of the best in the business, and the standard by which other designers' collections are measured. Then it grew into an even more enviable decorating business: this designer chooses her clients, not the other way around, and she doesn't choose many. To media mogul David Geffen, Rose Tarlow said yes, but to Microsoft founder Bill Gates, the answer was no.

Tarlow is the Madeleine Castaing of America, known for creating interiors that seem to sigh, with an uncanny appearance of age, beautifully patinaed woods, worn leather, poetic accessories, and warm tobacco tones serving as a kind of photo filter over everything. "The rooms that I like the most are the ones in old houses in England and France that have been there for centuries," said the designer, who is not afraid to employ old and sometimes complicated architectural and decorative elements, like the seventeenth-century limestone flooring she installed in one client's home, or the eleventh-century oak beams that adorn her own living room.

It was that living room, in her Bel Air house, that made Tarlow famous for an accessory unique in the history of decorating: a vine, which, after entering the interior through a cracked window, was encouraged to spread its tendrils up and over walls, and to dangle from the eight-hundred-year-old rafters—a romantic interlude that has since inspired a legion of Rose Tarlow imitators. Even the designer herself speaks in awe of her home's much-publicized beauty: "Sometimes I look out on the green lawn and I feel like I could faint."

Left Rose Tarlow once described her interiors as "soft and rambling, with a feeling that they'd been there forever." **Opposite** Bold scale, deep age, and heavy romanticism give Tarlow's work a singular atmosphere. **Overleaf** The room that made Tarlow a legend: her Bel Air living room, with its vine-covered walls and rafters.

GONE
TOO SOON

MICHAEL GREER

JAY SPECTRE

KALEF ALATON

ROBERT METZGER

HARRISON CULTRA

JED JOHNSON

GREG JORDAN

80 | Michael Greer
1916–1976

"Two of almost anything are better than one, provided one of it is better than none."

"A pyramid rising from a broad base of abominable, through gradually diminishing areas of acceptable, through still smaller areas of good, to a little point which is our truly excellent design." That's the highly quotable Michael Greer describing contemporary American design in his 1962 book, *Inside Design*, the most devilish ever written about decorating.

By the time his book was published, Greer had already established himself as a leading Manhattan decorator, with clients such as the actor Charlton Heston and the Eisenhower White House. He was an ardent Francophile, so passionate about French furniture that his friends called him Mr. Directoire. But it was *Inside Design*, an astringent romp through the fashions and foibles of interior design, that was his real claim to fame, introducing the opinionated Greer to a wider audience. Chintz, he advised, "is a family affair; some of the heart goes out of it in interiors inhabited by single people." Gag clocks, like cuckoos, he wrote, "never amuse and never fail to reflect on the intelligence and taste of anyone displaying them." It was caustic to be sure, but **his book offered some of the best decorating advice ever put on paper.**

Greer's triumphs were ultimately overshadowed by the circumstances of his death. Strangled by his personal assistant and found dead in his bed in a dressing gown, his ankles bound by a red sash, Greer became fodder for the media—an ignominious end to an impressive career. As feverishly written about as his murder was, so, too, was his exquisitely decorated Park Avenue apartment. Said one detective while investigating the murder, "It looked like a museum."

Above left Largely forgotten today, Michael Greer was one of America's foremost decorators in the mid-twentieth century. **Left** Although a traditionalist, believing that "there is so much to enjoy in the past," Greer would keep rooms up to date with intense colors. **Opposite** An ardent Francophile, Greer lavished his Park Avenue apartment with the French antiques he so admired.

81 | Jay Spectre
1929–1992

"I don't see any reason why a room has to be forever. It's more interesting when work documents a decade."

Rejecting the brown furniture and timid florals that prevailed in his native Kentucky, Jay Spectre followed the lead of many a Southern designer and reinvented himself in Manhattan. In time, he became more New York than most New Yorkers, with a uniquely modern style he dubbed "functional opulence."

"I was hell-bent on making a statement." And Spectre did, especially with his first Manhattan apartment, its walls sheathed in corrugated metal and its windows covered with galvanized-steel vertical blinds, supposedly the first of their kind in a residence. Eventually the designer settled into a softer point of view, in which chrome and brushed steel were juxtaposed with luxurious materials like parchment, mohair, and silk. He used them to cover walls and, sometimes, ceilings. In the 1970s and '80s his look was thoroughly of the moment, with the designer expressing little concern about how well it would—or wouldn't—age. "Some of my works may have been in style one year, out

the next," he said, "but whatever they were, they were never safe or boring."

Spectre wouldn't live to own a laptop or an iPhone, but he was **one of the first to anticipate the changing American home by embracing state-of-the-art technology rather than concealing it.** He claimed to have designed the first modern media room, and flaunted his clients' music systems and movie projectors by encasing them in steel and even crocodile, justifying his choices thusly: "To me, technology goes hand in hand with glamour."

Above Jay Spectre introduced glamour, luxury, and a whiff of Art Deco to seventies and eighties-era modernism. **Opposite** Spectre treated audio equipment and televisions sumptuously; for this client's sound system he created custom steel cabinetry. **Overleaf** Channel-quilted leather upholstery was a favorite of Spectre's, who used it liberally in his Manhattan apartment.

82 | Kalef Alaton
1940–1989

"The concept of combining styles is similar to acquiring friends. It's nice to have young friends and old friends."

K alef Alaton is remarkably forgotten today, though still quietly revered by a few of our most sophisticated designers, including Madeline Stuart and J. Randall Powers. Born in Turkey, then a resident of Paris for many years, he ultimately settled in Los Angeles and became one of its most celebrated design talents. He was central to the coming-of-age of California decorating and was responsible for introducing an urbane dimension to it.

His work frequently featured in *Architectural Digest*, Alaton was one of a coterie of California designers who achieved international fame in the 1970s and '80s thanks to the patronage of editor in chief Paige Rense and the growing success of her Los Angeles–based magazine, which at that time emphasized West Coast design. Houses featured in *AD* during that era had a distinctive sexy glamour, often photographed at night and accentuated with dramatic lighting, and Alaton's work was a perfect fit with that style.

Where Alaton differed from many of his California colleagues was his Continental point of view. Subtle colors typically provided a contemporary canvas for the antiques and ancient artifacts with which Alaton usually worked—he was especially fond of classical sculpture and gilded accents—while modern upholstered seating covered in solid fabrics blended easily into tightly edited surroundings. Nothing as mundane as a flat-screen TV, had they existed then, would ever have marred the walls of an Alaton room. "Everything is so much more focused when there are few distractions." It was all so deceptively simple; the reality was that his carefully curated rooms could take years to complete.

And then it all ended quickly and tragically. At age forty-nine, Kalef Alaton died of AIDS.

Above left Today he is considered something of a hidden gem: Kalef Alaton. **Opposite** Everything—a bust, a chest, a chair—was sculpture in an Alaton room. **Overleaf** Chinoiserie, French antiques, modern art, white walls, and gilding—Alaton's designs followed a decidedly California recipe.

83 | Robert Metzger
1940–1994

"I'm not afraid of mixing color,
I'm not afraid of scale,
I'm not afraid of drama."

Known for no one particular style but, instead, a whole host of them, Robert Metzger bounced around from Art Deco and Régence to Ch'ing Dynasty—sometimes all in one room. Stylistically voracious or just a compulsive shopper, Metzger indulged with confidence, believing that "it is death for a designer to be associated with only one look." But whatever direction they took, his interiors did have one thing in common: drama.

A poster boy of the 1980s, Metzger channeled the lavishness of the high-flying decade in his work. "We're living in the eighties, a fabulous era, so let's look it." That meant richly appointed and often opulent interiors for the record mogul Clive Davis and the fashion designer Carolina Herrera. Contemporary art and furniture shaped a Metzger interior, but antiques were the key. "There's nothing that softens a room, that creates a mood, a quality, a lifestyle, better than beautiful antique objects." Still it must be noted that Metzger also dabbled in some of the horrors of that era: overscaled upholstered furniture, strip lighting, and the color mauve.

"We're the Charlotte Russe, the extra cream" was how Metzger once described his profession. Sadly he would never get the opportunity to translate his style to subsequent decades: he died of AIDS-related pneumonia in 1994.

Above left Robert Metzger was a self-professed "compulsive buyer." **Left** His taste for mauve and indirect lighting seems démodé today, but during the 1970s and '80s, it earned Metzger a cadre of exclusive clients. **Opposite** Explaining his no-one-look look, epitomized by this multi-functional living room with billiard table, Metzger said, "I'm flexible but not wishy-washy."

84 | Harrison Cultra
1941–1983

"It's a big mistake to be a snob about inspiration."

"There is one answer to almost any question about decoration, and that is 'simplify.'" So said Harrison Cultra, **the most prominent traditionalist of the generation of young male designers lost to the AIDS epidemic.**

While others of his generation were rolling out commercial carpet and plain platform beds, Cultra preferred antiques and chintz, updating and modernizing them in visually slimmed-down environments. "People would be surprised at how dramatically their environs would change if they shipped half of everything they owned to the country." Elaborate curtains were never part of the Cultra vocabulary, but sisal rugs and contemporary seating usually were. If there were emphatic moments, they likely involved color: he was known to paint walls pink or spring green. And when it came to accessories, the bigger, the better. They were chosen for their ability to stand up to a room's architecture, not scaled down to insignificance. As Cultra made known, his interiors contained "no collections of little gold boxes."

Like many designers, Cultra had a talent for turning his own house into a stream of publicity. At Teviotdale, his eighteenth-century house on the Hudson River, he had the opportunity to work with the three things he loved best: "lots of promising raw material, civilized clients, and—architecture!"

Opposite After getting his start with Rose Cumming Inc., Harrison Cultra made his name decorating for Jacqueline Onassis and Richard Jenrette. **Below** The living room at his country house, Teviotdale in Germantown, New York, was a prime example of Cultra's edited approach to traditional design; note the bare windows.

85 | Jed Johnson
1948–1996

"I learned about design through shopping."

Jed Johnson spent the years leading up to his design career sweeping floors at Andy Warhol's Factory before becoming the artist's companion and collaborator, eventually directing the cult-classic film *Andy Warhol's Bad* in 1977. Although one might think that spending time among Ultra Violet and Candy Darling would influence Johnson's aesthetic in outrageous ways, his decorating was anything but outré, and was in fact renowned for its dignity.

Lacking a formal design education but blessed with an eye for quality, Johnson got his training working on the Upper East Side townhouse that he shared with Warhol for many years. A student of the decorative arts, he advised Warhol on his collections of Art Deco and American Federal pieces, displaying them against a sympathetic, elegant background of stenciled walls and sober colors. **Warhol's treasure house defied expectations and made Johnson's career, sending him quickly down the** path to becoming one of America's top designers, with A-list clients such as Mick Jagger, Pierre Bergé, and Richard Gere.

Despite the lofty circles he traveled in, Johnson retained a low-key presence that suggested extreme shyness. His normal speaking voice was barely a whisper; you would have to get uncomfortably close just to hear him. But it was all part of a unique and very attractive mystique. And then, at the peak of his career, it all ended in a shocking instant with the explosion of TWA Flight 800. He was only forty-seven.

Opposite Self-taught, Jed Johnson became an accomplished designer and furniture expert, two skills that buoyed him to the top. **Below** Johnson took particular delight in collecting Arts and Crafts furniture, which he assembled in his Manhattan duplex.

86 | Greg Jordan
1957–2005

"Today everything has to have a purpose. There aren't a lot of clients we buy marble grapes for."

Like many who move to New York, Greg Jordan came to write the great American novel. But in a plot twist worthy of fiction, Jordan instead became an in-demand designer of the 1990s and one of the freshest faces of the decade. His all-American manner came through not just in his decorating, but in his down-to-earth personality: "It's not all about poufs and chintz. Rooms that can't be lived in seem silly."

Ginghams, toiles, and even the same floral-print wallpaper that appeared in Aunt Pittypat's house in *Gone with the Wind*—these were just some of the traditional patterns that Jordan resuscitated, zipping them up with shots of color or modernizing them in neutrals. Avoiding the heavy hand that had plagued some of his colleagues during the previous decade, he explained, "We are moving away from overly adorned decorating. The trend is toward elegant rooms that are simple and to the point."

Like a Thin Man movie, Jordan's work crackled with wit, never more so than in his own two-room Manhattan apartment, where walls, windows, and upholstery were covered with a chain-link print that Jordan likened to "an urban version of an eighteenth-century trellis print." After a successful run in New York, he became bi-coastal, bringing his East Coast chic to Los Angeles, where it seemed even more perfect. Until his untimely death, the sky seemed the limit for him.

Above His looks and attire were straight-laced, but Greg Jordan's interiors had many a twist. Opposite Jordan's playful side was evident in his New York City apartment, which he enveloped in a custom-designed chain-link-patterned fabric. Overleaf Even when the curtains were grand, Jordan knew how to take things down a notch—by introducing pink-and-white cotton gingham.

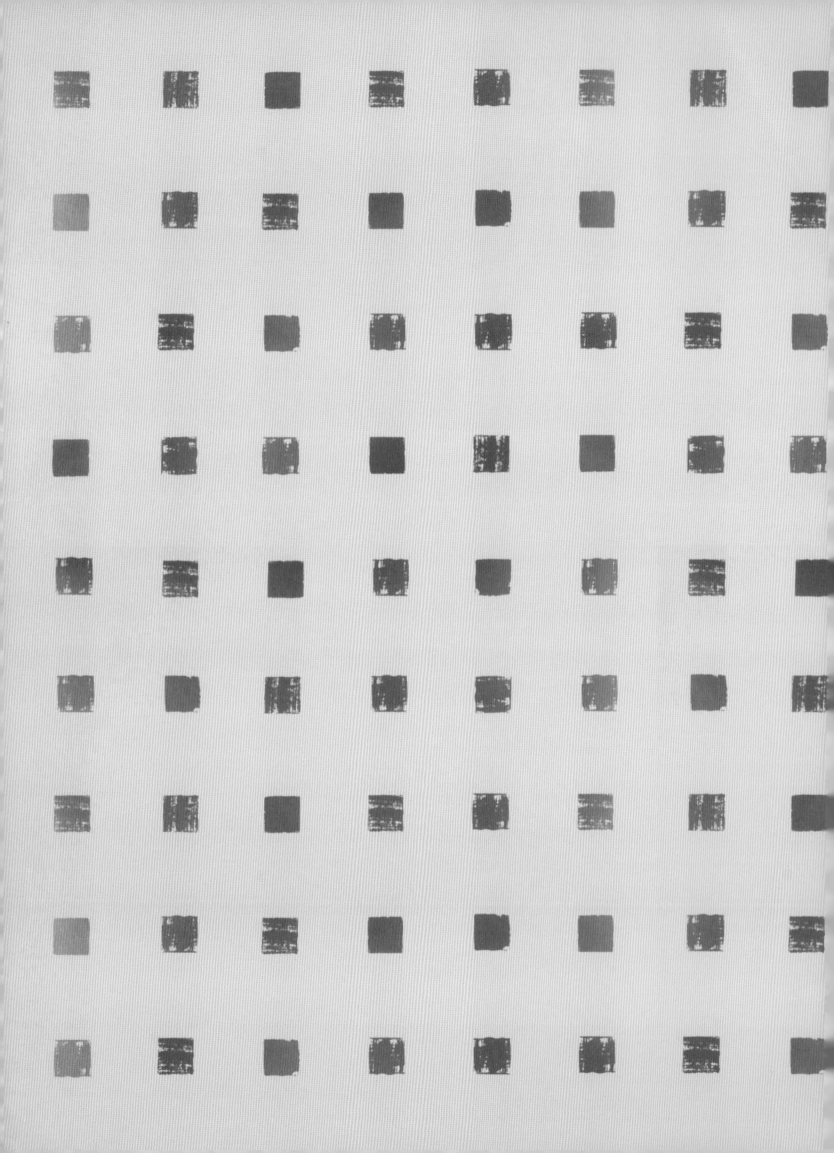

MAKING THEIR MARK

DAVID KLEINBERG

DANIEL ROMUALDEZ

BRIAN McCARTHY

PETER DUNHAM

INDIA MAHDAVI

BRUCE BUDD

MICHAEL SMITH

PIERRE YOVANOVITCH

KELLY WEARSTLER

MARKHAM ROBERTS

STEVEN GAMBREL

MILES REDD

ALEXA HAMPTON

JEAN-LOUIS DENIOT

87 | David Kleinberg
1954–

"I like to think that my name comes to mind when someone wants a timeless, tranquil interior."

Considering that David Kleinberg did a stint working for Denning and Fourcade—the duo that enraptured high society with their opulent ways—followed by sixteen years alongside the doyenne of WASP decorating, Sister Parish, one would expect his solo career to be defined by chintz and poufs. In fact, it's quite the opposite. **At heart a minimalist, Kleinberg has conquered American design with a style he describes as "architectural and masculine and pared down."**

From Denning and Fourcade, Kleinberg received "my first exposure to the good life, and I was enthralled," while from Sister Parish he learned "how a house should run, how people live in it, how people entertain." Both lessons proved valuable, ensuring that no matter how much restraint Kleinberg may exert over a room—and make no mistake, restrained it is—its comfort and livability are never diminished. A Kleinberg interior begs to host a fabulous party as much as it invites sitting alone and reading a book.

Not as nostalgic as a Parish-Hadley interior, but not quite ready to part company with traditionalism either, Kleinberg's work represents a forward-thinking way of decorating without losing sight of the past. Although he was describing himself, Kleinberg's self-assessment could apply to his work, too: "I think of myself as a classical person, but a classical person in the modern world."

Left Grounded in traditional design, David Kleinberg has created his own modern adaptation of it. **Opposite** For this Upper East Side dining room, Kleinberg stepped out on his usual neutral color palette by covering chairbacks in an array of sorbet shades. **Overleaf** The designer's own prewar apartment in Manhattan sums up his masculine—and very refined—style.

88 | Daniel Romualdez
1960–

> "I really believe you're only as good as your client. I've learned so much from working with the stylish women that I do."

Until recently Daniel Romualdez was a well-kept secret of sorts—a secret password for a high-profile clientele that included some of Manhattan's most influential women. But one client in particular helped to let the secret out, pushing Romualdez to the head of the pack and landing him the biggest publicity coup of all, and a rare one for a decorator: a feature in *Vanity Fair*.

Having trained under Peter Marino and Robert A.M. Stern before opening his own firm, Romualdez had his breakthrough moment courtesy of the clothing designer Tory Burch, who considers him "a master at taking people's taste and making it better." His first brush with fame was Burch's apartment at the Pierre in New York, whose moss-green velvet walls and yellow-lacquered library were chronicled in *Vogue*. But **it was Romualdez's work on the then-fledgling network of Tory Burch stores that clinched his reputation.** Slick, yet preppy, they were a David Hicks–like mix of gleaming walls, brass-trimmed shelving, and plenty of Burch's favorite color:

orange. It was a winning combination that was ripe for knockoffs, of which, in fact, there have been many.

Aesthetically versatile—or, in his own words, "schizophrenic"—Romualdez skillfully toils in any number of styles, the full range being evident in his own many residences. Of those, the most prominent has to be his Connecticut home, a onetime eighteenth-century tavern whose previous occupant was also famous for his eye: the fashion designer Bill Blass.

Opposite Daniel Romualdez cultivates an air of mystery unique for the design world; he has neither a business website nor a social media presence. **Below** Romualdez's breakout moment came when *Vogue* featured his design of Tory Burch's apartment at the Pierre, its library lacquered a zesty shade of yellow. **Overleaf** The designer excels at taking traditional fabrics, like this Tree of Life, and making them feel new, as he did in a bedroom of his Connecticut house.

89

Brian McCarthy

1960–

> "If you don't lay the groundwork, if you don't get that foundation, you're never going to be that good—or as good as you aspire to be."

Rising through the ranks of Parish-Hadley—which sometimes meant mixing Sister's signature vodka-and-Clamato-juice cocktail—Brian McCarthy credits his time spent working alongside Albert Hadley with shaping his informed point of view and honing the skills he needed to strike out on his own later. Unfailingly appreciative of those formative years, McCarthy, along with fellow alum Bunny Williams, recently compiled a best-selling history of the firm, *Parish-Hadley Tree of Life*.

Astonishingly versatile, McCarthy does not have "a look" he imposes on his multitude of projects. His interiors can be crisp and modern, with tailored furnishings and contemporary art that bear some trace of Hadley's influence. Or they can just as successfully go historical, as in one Atlanta townhouse that, if one didn't know better, one might assume was an eighteenth-century *hôtel particulier* in Paris.

Head and shoulders above the crowd in terms of his work's high-caliber detail and craftsmanship, McCarthy continues the tradition established long ago by the design greats. "You have to have a reference for excellence," McCarthy asserts, "and we certainly got that at Parish-Hadley." Working with a kind of luxury rare for today, McCarthy has been known to indulge in custom Chinese-lacquer panels in one room and *verre églomisé* in the next—in other words, "the richness and subtlety that elevates an interior from the well done to the magical."

Left Like several designers in this book, Brian McCarthy is one of Parish-Hadley Associates' high-profile graduates. **Opposite** Extraordinary detailing is a defining feature of McCarthy's work; here, custom-crafted, gilded mahogany paneling and a Louis XIV–inspired painted ceiling. **Overleaf** McCarthy's own Manhattan apartment, with its array of styles and furnishings, does not "speak a single language."

90

Peter Dunham

1961–

"Reverting to a safe, matchy-matchy story is a mistake. It starts to look less interesting, and more like a '70s or '80s hotel."

His English accent does not even begin to tell his story. Peter Dunham was raised in France by a French-American father and an English mother. He spent summers in Spain. He was educated in England, where his interest in interior design led to an internship with David Hicks, the father of his school friend Ashley. Alas, after being warned off the profession by both Hicks and Jacques Grange, who told Dunham it was a difficult way to make a living, he took a more sensible route: selling real estate in Manhattan. He then came to Los Angeles in 1998, where flipping houses led him full circle to interior design and his present career as one of the West Coast's most successful interior designers. **Adding his own special worldliness to the casual attitude of Southern California, Dunham has found the ideal landscape for a free-spirited global style.**

Having once been described as Merchant Ivory Moderne, Dunham's look reflects both his English roots and his love of travel, especially to places like India and the Middle East. In the English way, it's very loose. "I like to mix things," he says, "so they look thrown together rather than overcalculated." His particular signature is his enthusiastic use of exotic and tribal-patterned fabrics, many of which are of his own adaptations. The fabrics, along with cushions, furniture, and all manner of accessories, are sold at his expansive Los Angeles shop, Hollywood at Home, which is something of a hit factory. His How to Marry a Millionaire chair, a raffia-wrapped version of a Robsjohn-Gibbings design, has become a modern classic.

As stylish as they may be, Dunham's interiors are, above all else, relaxed. After twenty years in Los Angeles, he has many quintessentially Californian attitudes: "It's a buzzkill to be careful every time one sits in a chair or puts a drink down on the table. That doesn't mean giving up on style."

Left Peter Dunham is a unique mix of European and American sensibilities. Opposite "I like houses that look relatively accumulated," says Dunham, who has a particular fondness for exotic textiles and mid-century furniture. Overleaf In Dunham's own living room, a pair of his How to Marry a Millionaire chairs, covered in his Fig Leaf fabric.

91 | India Mahdavi
1962–

"My work is about happiness."

Shaped by her global upbringing, which began in Tehran, Paris-based India Mahdavi describes her taste as "polyglot and polychrome—a rich mix of cultures and colors." Steeped in stringent minimalism while artistic director at Christian Liaigre, Mahdavi went on to find her own voice. Now at the helm of her own firm, with commercial and residential work making her one of today's hottest European designers, **Mahdavi has crafted her own bold style of modernism that has made strong color and whimsy into status symbols.**

"What I am trying to do is to bring joy to people's lives," Mahdavi has said of her work, which has become famous for its chromatic daring. Whether at the Gallery at Sketch, the London restaurant that Mahdavi lavished in bubble-gum pink, or in her clients' homes, where she's not afraid to put "colors in danger," the designer has given sophisticates license to move beyond understatement and have some fun. Still, it should be said that she is just as apt to employ neutrals—when a room calls for it—tailoring each of her projects so that they are "like couture pieces."

Having been "influenced by American pop culture, cartoons, and Walt Disney movies"—she absorbed all three as a child in Cambridge, Massachusetts—Mahdavi admits "there is something cartoony about my work." It's a quality best seen in her much-touted furniture designs, whose originality and playfulness have earned them places in the world's most buzzed-about hotels, restaurants, and boîtes.

Above After years of neutral shades ruling interior design, India Mahdavi put color back into play with her dynamic style. **Opposite** Having once worked for Christian Liaigre, Mahdavi understands clean, strong lines and neutrals, too, here in a Connecticut home. **Overleaf** A high-octane Paris loft is proof that no color combination is too daring for Mahdavi.

92 | Bruce Budd

1964–

> "Decorating is a bit like shooting a film or writing a novel."

Imagine decorating a Connecticut showhouse room early in one's profession and, as a result, **earning the support, admiration, and patronage of three icons of American taste: fashion designer Bill Blass, interior designer Albert Hadley, and socialite Bunny Mellon.** No fantasy, this was the first bloom of Bruce Budd's design career, which started out in the 1990s on the highest possible note.

Budd is best known for having worked exclusively for Mellon, who died in 2014. She was his first client, and in addition to having decorated her many houses, he lives in a carriage house in Manhattan she owned. With a distinctive style echoing that of his patroness, Budd prefers to decorate with humble materials, such as coarse, natural-fiber rugs and cotton and linen fabrics. Chic, and sober. As admiring as he is of clean-lined and sometimes spare antiques, he is equally a fan of contemporary furniture and art that give the designer's work the sense of being current. And yet it is timeless, too. A comparison to Billy Baldwin wouldn't be wrong.

Although his work for Mellon was rarely published—she was notoriously press-shy—Budd managed to cut an impressive figure in the design world in part because of his association with her. Once known to only a few, Budd has since expanded his clientele and even garnered media coverage, earning him an increasingly prominent role in American design.

Left It was his role as socialite Bunny Mellon's decorator that made Bruce Budd the envy of the design world. **Opposite** Albert Hadley once described Budd's style as "all about shape and sculpture," evident here in the designer's residence, a converted carriage house in Manhattan. **Overleaf** Reminiscent of Billy Baldwin, Budd excels at mixing modern pieces with antiques, then toning everything down with something humble, like rush matting.

93 | Michael Smith

1964–

"People think California is all guacamole and Eames furniture, but we have a big tradition of pretty houses, too."

With his streaked blond hair and a predilection for wearing trainers, Los Angeles–based Michael Smith is the walking definition of West Coast insouciance. But beneath his laid-back facade is a disciplined designer so attentive to his work he was tasked with the ultimate challenge: decorating the Obama White House, the most fraught assignment of them all.

As the Los Angeles designer William Haines did long before him, **Smith made his name catering to Hollywood's power players, furnishing their homes with his relaxed manner of traditional decorating—not quite Spanish, not quite English, not quite French, but unmistakably Californian.** (Smith has something else in common with Haines as well: he recently designed the spectacular new visitors' center at Sunnylands, the former Annenberg residence, considered Haines's masterpiece.) But Smith has since moved well beyond Hollywood. Now just as much a presence on the East Coast as he is in Europe—he recently redecorated the US Embassy residence in Madrid, where his partner served as ambassador—Smith is internationally recognized as one of America's top designers.

Yet Smith has not ventured far from his California roots, which, in recent years, he has interpreted in an increasingly modern way. Nowhere is this better seen than in his weekend residence near Palm Springs, a 1970s version of the Mayan Revival style. Flush with travertine and loaded with stellar examples of twentieth-century furniture, the house represents a desert oasis of refinement to its owner. "For me," he says, "this house is that idea of Southern California as a very sophisticated place."

Left Laid-back on the surface, Michael Smith is highly driven, with an international clientele and multiple product collections to his name. **Opposite** In recent years, Smith's work has assumed a more modern sensibility, expressed full tilt in the family room of his Rancho Mirage, California, house. **Overleaf** Smith made his name with a traditional, but casual, style that incorporated English, Spanish, and American influences.

94 | Pierre Yovanovitch
1965–

"If I listened to my true self, I'd live with nothing but white walls and a bench."

Describing his own work as "monk-like but comfortable," the Frenchman Pierre Yovanovitch **continues the spirit of thirties design legend and fellow countryman, Jean-Michel Frank.** Like Frank, Yovanovitch has made his name creating ascetic yet luxurious interiors that reflect "the spirit of French design. Very chic, but restrained. Minimal in its way, but still warm."

Forgoing an earlier career designing menswear for Pierre Cardin, Yovanovitch is self-taught in interior design. Yet since opening his firm in 2001, he has more than proven his mettle, garnering fashion heavyweights Christian Louboutin and François-Henri Pinault as clients. Not overly concerned with decorations—"useless ornament must give way to the essential"—the designer places his emphasis on interior architecture, so much so that he employs mostly architects at his firm, explaining, "I thought I'd set myself apart by giving priority to the volumes rather than to the decoration."

As edited as his style is, Yovanovitch can get excited about furniture, as long as it possesses the same strong, simple lines of his interiors. Particularly fond of mid-century American and Scandinavian pieces, he shows special preference for the furniture designs of James Mont, Edward Wormley, Vladimir Kagan, and, more recently, himself. Having launched a collection that melds minimalism with playfulness—his popular Papa Bear chair looks just as you'd imagine—Yovanovitch, who admits to being highly ambitious, has now set his sights on America, though not to the abandonment of his native France. "Americans," he says, "give you the kind of fuel the French don't."

Opposite Pierre Yovanovitch characterizes his work as "luxury devoid of ostentation." **Above left** Twentieth-century furniture by Paul Frankl and James Mont offers a striking contrast to the seventeenth-century architecture of Yovanovitch's own French château. **Left** Favorite designs, like the Flemming Lassen chair in the corner of this room, appear often in the designer's interiors. **Overleaf** Stone and wood, which the designer calls "noble" materials, figure prominently in his work.

95 | Kelly Wearstler
1967–

> "As a designer, I'm always evolving and getting more confident—and sassy."

Responsible for the Hollywood Regency revival craze that swept America as the century turned, Los Angeles–based Kelly Wearstler became the face of glamorous decorating for the new millennium, earning her a cult status rare in interior design. It shows no signs of waning.

After the beige nineties, Wearstler burst onto the scene in dramatic fashion, brandishing bold colors, fabulous mid-century furniture, and strong patterns last seen in the early 1970s. Graphic black and white frequently set the scene, further enlivened with splashy color. Attention-getting accessories were a cornerstone of the Wearstler look, especially those now-ubiquitous life-size ceramic dogs.

Just as the theatricality of the thirties-era Regency Revival played into the early years of magazine photography, Wearstler's work was the kind of photogenic decorating that seemed made for blogging, whose nascent days coincided with those of her career. An early darling of the blogosphere, Wearstler became a household name largely because of social media and her appearance as a judge on one of television's earliest design-oriented reality shows, Bravo's *Top Design*, where she was known for her fashion-forward, and sometimes eccentric, wardrobe and hair. In one episode, she donned a lofty turban.

When the Hollywood Regency look peaked, Wearstler moved on to sleeker pastures, but not before decorating a string of resort hotels, whose made-for-the-camera interiors once again garnered a slew of media coverage. So, too, did her association with the Manhattan luxury department store Bergdorf Goodman, where she not only has her own boutique, but also decorated the restaurant, BG. Its eggshell-blue leather porter's chairs are the most coveted seats in the store.

Left Kelly Wearstler has a reputation for being fearless when it comes to both design and fashion. **Opposite** Wearstler made her glamorous rendition of a French porter's chair the must-have chair of the last decade. **Overleaf** For the living room at her Hillcrest Estate, the designer turned up the volume of every element.

96 | Markham Roberts
1967–

"At the end of the day, you want a place that's calm."

Rooms artfully arranged to foster easy living and entertaining; well-bred fabrics; prime real estate afforded to small tables meant to hold drinks—these were once the hallmarks of gracious living, and they still describe the work of Markham Roberts, today's torchbearer for classic American style. **Roberts is known for blowing the dust off traditional furnishings, stripping them of their dowager quality, and making them exciting once again.**

He continues to use old-fashioned chintzes and toiles, for example, that become contemporary when partnered with snappy colors and the right accessories. The same goes for that onetime stalwart of the living room: the game table, which Roberts has revived, nurturing the next generation of bridge players. Always he makes it a point not to get stuck in the past: "I certainly don't want to live like my grandmother. I want to put my feet up and watch a flat-screen TV."

Roberts's other strength is his attention to detail, ranging from brown walls lacquered so beautifully they look like melted chocolate, to custom-designed furniture painted to look like animal horn. But as richly satisfying as Roberts's work is, its greatest virtue is its lack of ostentation. Roberts, a native of Indianapolis, brings a Midwestern practicality to his profession. No matter how glossy the paint job, he couldn't be flashy if he tried.

Opposite Having grown up in gracious surroundings, Markham Roberts is a favorite of young social types accustomed to well-mannered homes. **Below** Skilled at using every square inch of a room effectively, Roberts typically supplies enough seating for a crowd. **Overleaf** Roberts's particular gift is the impossible trick of using strong color—walls lacquered sapphire, Tiffany-blue lampshades—to understated effect.

97 | Steven Gambrel
1969–

"It's all about living in the now instead of weighing myself down with nostalgia."

What Mario Buatta and Mark Hampton were to the eighties, today it's Steven Gambrel: the status-symbol designer for young titans of finance and technology. But whereas Buatta and Hampton set out to legitimize their clients' newly elevated places in society with richly appointed traditionalism, Gambrel gives his clientele something very different: a defiant, modern swagger.

Gone are the Old Master paintings once favored by Saul Steinberg and his fellow Masters of the Universe. For Gambrel's clients, it is contemporary art that sends their pulses racing, especially when Gambrel pairs it with the customized wall finishes for which he is famous: bronzed mirror, cerused oak, molten glass, and always luxe. And the English antiques that were once de rigueur? Those, too, are missing, replaced by Prouvé and Ponti and the other mid-century classics that have become a hallmark of Gambrel's work. Among this generation of moguls, Chippendale and Boulle don't stand a chance.

Although known as a modernist, Gambrel has not entirely rejected tradition; after all, he has an architecture degree from Thomas Jefferson's temple, the University of Virginia. Introducing the softening effect of antique furniture or classical architectural details to interiors when appropriate, he tries to take a humanistic approach even to cutting-edge design, explaining, "The people who hire me have built their fortunes in finance or technology because they are attuned to what is happening today. But they don't want to build some sort of modernist rocket-ship house."

Left Steven Gambrel, the designer of choice to many of today's young tycoons. **Opposite** Strong modern shapes and unusual colors—a Gambrel room is not for the faint of heart. **Overleaf** Schooled in architecture, the designer pays as much attention to the bones of a room as he does to its furnishings.

Miles Redd

1969–

"I like to push the envelope—but just to the edge."

Born in Atlanta with a Southerner's innate love of everything home, Miles Redd approaches decorating with a fashion eye. Luxurious fabrics, trims, wall-coverings, furniture, and, above all, color define his stimulating world. After early years spent working for that design-world power couple Bunny Williams and John Rosselli, Redd eventually went solo, creating interiors of such spectacle **he has become the showman of American decorating.**

He prefers to be called a decorator, not the more modern, somewhat inflated "interior designer." A traditionalist at heart, he is a self-described "magpie," drawn to shiny things like lacquered walls, mirrored surfaces, and metallic wallpapers. Baroque flourishes, too, usually in the form of chalky-white William Kent–style tables, plaster urns, and ornate carved mirrors.

But Redd is synonymous with color, and doesn't hesitate to pack many strong hues into one house because, "I love color relationships more than anything else." The volume is turned up so high in his interiors that they proved photographic gold, among the most sought out by magazines. A dazzling monograph, *The Big Book of Chic*, and a furniture and accessories collection for Ballard Designs have only burnished his reputation.

Redd's inspirations are far-reaching and include 1930s cinema, European literature, French history, and famous twentieth-century aesthetes. It's the latter group to which Redd seems spiritually connected—he's a twenty-first-century successor to the group of design merrymakers that included Oliver Messel and Cecil Beaton.

Above Miles Redd: Glamour is his middle name.
Opposite Leather upholstered doors, nailhead trim, and black-and-white floors are three decorative threads that run throughout his work. **Overleaf** No easy feat, Redd successfully packs a staggering array of strong colors into this room.

99 | Alexa Hampton

1971–

"I am an underground formal person. I'm so outgoing, gregarious and silly and bawdy, but my work isn't."

She is design royalty—her father was none other than Mark Hampton. Alexa Hampton learned her trade from the very best, starting her training with him at the age of thirteen, and assuming the reins of Mark Hampton LLC when she was only twenty-seven. **The loss of the founder is a transition most firms fail to make, but Hampton emerged from her father's shadow as a talented designer in her own right, shepherding the family firm into the twenty-first century while remaining loyal to his design principles.** "I have no interest in defying his style," she said. "I think he was, and is, a genius."

A child of the 1980s and a mother to young children, Hampton bridges the gap between the decorous environments in which she and her clients were raised and today's desire for informal living. "A lot of younger people love what our parents had but maybe don't want to be so traditional," Hampton has said. "We have fewer layers, and we're less wedded to being rigorously partial to one particular period." Hampton has made it a habit of giving her clients the best of both worlds: homes that are dressed up just enough for special occasions but, with their practical layouts and comfortable furnishings, easier to live with from day to day.

She has licensed a range of products, including fabrics, lighting, fireplace mantels, and a furniture collection for Hickory Chair, which made its first licensing agreement with her father back in 1988. A devoted neoclassicist and one of today's most erudite designers, Hampton also carries on yet one more family tradition: a very quick wit.

Left Now at the helm of her late father's firm, Alexa Hampton has updated his traditional style for the twenty-first century. **Opposite** Although Hampton's work is comfortable and, at times, casual, the designer still maintains respect for elegantly appointed dining and living rooms. **Overleaf** Hampton's own taste runs toward neoclassicism and souvenirs of the Grand Tour; here, her Manhattan living room.

100 | Jean-Louis Deniot

1974–

"Luxury is when it seems flawless and not contrived."

Although he is thought of as the quintessential modernist, France's most recognizable young designer, Jean-Louis Deniot, has a special reverence for the past. "I don't do pure contemporary," he says, "as in my mind, it has no soul. I need to have history in my work."

He has a gift for instilling a sense of exactness in his spaces, though never at the cost of ambience. "I always want to get as far as possible away from the white box," he says. "My interiors are about atmosphere, character, texture, and a sense of harmony." More than anything they are unmistakably French: the futuristic energy; the cerebral quality; the luxurious finishes, like parchment, calling to mind the work of his predecessor Jean-Michel Frank; the fabulous twentieth-century French furniture from the finest Left Bank shops, by blue-chip designers like Arbus, Poillerat, and Adnet.

Inevitably he is now working a great deal in America, too, where he recently debuted a furniture collection for Baker. **Like Stéphane Boudin before him, Deniot has redefined Frenchness.**

Left The wunderkind of French design, Jean-Louis Deniot attained international fame while in his thirties. **Opposite** Rich, urbane hues and outstanding modernist furniture are bedrocks of Deniot's interiors. **Overleaf** Equally enthralled by the past and present, Deniot loves "the purity of modernism, but I also appreciate the previous millennia of architecture." For an apartment on Avenue Foch in Paris, Deniot included many examples of mid-century modern furniture, a hallmark of his work.

ACKNOWLEDGMENTS

A book of this magnitude (a whopping 100 designers spanning 100 years) can only be tackled by a hard-working team of individuals. I would like to thank Mark Magowan, Beatrice Vincenzini, and Francesco Venturi, who threw Vendome's full support behind this project, as well as the team at Kravet. Special thanks to Jim Spivey, Celia Fuller, Vivien Hamley, and David Shannon, whose Herculean efforts resulted in a book of which I am immensely proud. I would also like to acknowledge the expertise provided by Vendome's publicist, Meghan Phillips, and William Clark, my very capable agent. I mustn't forget to call out the busy magazine editors who graciously provided me with quotes for this book: Amy Astley, Michael Boodro, Sophie Donelson, Marian McEvoy, Lisa Newsom, Nancy Novogrod, Whitney Robinson, Clinton Smith, and Newell Turner.

My debt of gratitude to my editor, Stephen Drucker, continues to grow. A decade after giving me my first big break as a contributing editor to *House Beautiful* magazine, Stephen continues to be my champion, and for that I will always be grateful.

Most of all, I would like to thank every designer who has toiled in the interior design profession. I am in awe of your skill and talent, which has made the past century of design a dazzling one.

PHOTOGRAPHY CREDITS

Pages ii, 128–29, 131, 284: Photos © 2018 Russell MacMasters Photography | Page vi: Photo © 2018 William Waldron | Pages 2, 4: Photos © 2018 Mattie E. Hewitt & Richard A. Smith Photograph Collection/New York Historical Society | Pages 3, 11, 14–15, 16, 17, 93, 94, 116–17, 127, 156, 205: Photos © 2018 Horst P. Horst/Condé Nast via Getty | Page 6: Photo © 2018 Centre Pompidou, MNAM-CCI, Dist. RMN-Grand Palais / image Centre Pompidou, MNAM-CCI | Page 7: Photo © 2018 Centre Pompidou, MNAM-CCI, Dist. RMN-Grand Palais /Man Ray Trust/Artists Rights Society (ARS), NY/ADAGP Paris 2018 | Pages 8–9, 216 (bottom): Photos © 2018 Esto/Ezra Stoller | Page 10: Photo © 2018 Billy Cunningham/Architectural Digest/Condé Nast | Pages 11, 96–97, 133: Photos © 2018 Horst P. Horst/Architectural Digest/Condé Nast | Pages 18–19, 249, 336–337: Photos © 2018 Oberto Gili/House & Garden/Condé Nast | Pages 22, 141, 256–57, 296–97: Photos © 2018 Michael Mundy/Condé Nast | Pages 23, 270, 326–27: Photos © 2018 Fernando Bengoechea/Condé Nast | Pages 24–25: Photo © 2018 William P Steele | Pages 26, 28–29, 30: Photo © 2018 The Estate of David Hicks | Page 27: Photo © 2018 Victor Watts/Alamy Stock Photo | Page 31: Photo © 2018 Pierre Berdoy | Page 34 (top): Photo © 2018 David Mode Payne/Condé Nast | Page 34 (bottom): Photo © 2018, courtesy of Jennifer Carlquist | Page 35: Photo courtesy Mattie E. Hewitt and Richard A. Smith Photograph Collection, New York Historical Society | Page 36 (top): Photo © 2018 Berenice Abbott/Commerce Graphics Ltd | Pages 36 (bottom), 37 (top): Photo © 2018 Museum of Ireland | Page 37 (bottom): Photo © 2018 The Museum of Modern Art/Licensed by SCALA / Art Resource, NY | Pages 38, 84, 88, 90–91, 157: Photos © 2018 The Cecil Beaton Studio Archive at Sotheby's | Page 39: Photo © 2018 Chronicle/Alamy Stock Photo | Pages 40–41: Photo © 2018 Historic England | Page 42: Photo © 2018 Library of Congress/AIA Library and Archives | Pages 43, 112–13: Photos © 2018 Gottscho-Schleisner Collection, Library of Congress | Pages 44–45: Photo © 2018 Samuel H. Gottscho/Condé Nast via Getty Images | Pages 46, 48–49: Photos © 2018 Collection of Sarah Cumming Cecil | Page 47: Photo © 2018 Estate of Jeanloup Sieffe/Maconochie | Page 50: Photo © 2018 Granger | Page 51: Photo © 2018 Pedro E.Guerrero/House & Garden/Condé Nast | Pages 52, 53, 290: Photos © 2018 images courtesy of Dorothy Draper and Company, Inc. | Pages 54–55: Photo © 2018 Metropolitan Museum of Art. Image source: Art Resource New York | Pages 56 (top), 57, 58–59: Photos © 2018 courtesy of McMillen Inc. | Page 60: Photo © 2018 Erica Lennard | Pages 61, 78 (bottom), 92, 95, 97, 164, 165, 167, 179, 180–81, 212 (top), 259: Photos © 2018 Derry Moore | Pages 62–63: Photo © 2018 Sotheby's/Art Digital Studio | Pages 64, 66, 67: Photos © 2018 Deidi von Schaewen | Pages 65, 230–31: Photo © 2018 Ivan Terestchenko | Page 68 (top): Photo © 2018 Gene Maggio/The New York Times | Pages 70, 335: Photos © 2018 Miguel Flores-Vianna | Pages 71, 72–73, 148–49, 252, 331, 332–33: Photo © 2018 Pieter Estersohn/Art Department | Page 74 (top): Photos © 2018 Barbara Barry/Reinerlight | Page 74 (bottom), 75: Photo © 2018 Matthew Millman/Architectural Digest/Condé Nast | Page 78 (top): Photo © 2018 George C. Beresford/Getty Images | Page 79: Photo © 2018 Historia/Rex/Shutterstock | Pages 80, 81: Photo © 2018 Courtesy of the Winterthur Library: Winterthur Archives | Page 82: Photo © 2018 Hulton Archive/Getty Images | Page 83: Photo © 2018 Clarence Sinclair Bull via John Kobal | Page 85: Photo © 2018 Pascal Hinous/Architectural Digest/Condé Nast | Page 86–87: Photo © 2018 Architectural Review/© F.L.C. / ADAGP, Paris / Artists Rights Society (ARS), New York | Page 89: Photo © 2018 Paul Popper/Popperfoto/Getty Images | Page 96: Photo © 2018 David Montgomery/Vogue/Condé Nast | Page 102: Photo © 2018 Center for Creative Photography | Page 103: Photo © 2018 Peter Nyholm/Condé Nast via Getty Images | Pages 104–5: Mrs. Kersey Coates Reed Residence, Lake Forest, IL. Adler and Work, architect. David Adler; courtesy of the Ryerson & Burnham Archives | Pages 106, 107, 108–9: Photo courtesy of the Hagley Museum & Library | Page 110: Photo © 2018 Anthony Denney/Vogue/Condé Nast | Page 111: Photo © 2018 John Rawlings/Condé Nast via Getty Images | Page 114: Photo © 2018 Parsons School of Design. Alumni Association; Wilbur Pippin. The New School Archives and Special Collection, The New School, New York, NY. | Page 115: Photo © 2018 John T. Hill | Page 118: Photo © 2018 Haanel Cassidy/Condé Nast via Getty Images | Page 119: Photo © 2018 Loomis Dean/The LIFE Picture Collection/Getty | Pages 120–21: Photo © 2018 Maynard L. Parker, photographer. Courtesy of The Huntington Library, San Marino, California | Page 120: Photo © 2018 Michael Pateman | Page 121: Photo © 2018 Jaime Ardiles-Arce | Pages 124–25, 300–1: Photos © 2018 Peter Aaron/Otto | Pages 126, 285: Photo © 2018 Fred Lyon/Condé Nast | Page 130: Photo © 2018 Jim McHugh | Pages 132, 142: Photo © 2018 Mary E. Nicols for Architectural Digest | Pages 134–35: Photo © 2018 Charles S. White/Architectural Digest/Condé Nast | Page 136: Photo © 2018 Donghia, Inc. | Page 137: Photo © 2018 Angelo Donghia/Architectural Digest/Condé Nast | Pages 138–39, 218–19, 311, 319: Photos © 2018 Jaime Ardiles-Arce/Architectural Digest/Condé Nast | Page 140: Photo courtesy of Vicente Wolf | Pages 143, 338: Photos © 2018 Joshua McHugh | Page 144–45: Photo © 2018 Thibault Jeanson, courtesy of Stephen Sills | Pages 146, 147, 366: Photo © 2018 Francesco Lagnese/Otto | Page 152: Photo © 2018 Country Life Picture Library | Pages 153, 154: Illustration © 2018 W.E. Ranken/World of Interiors | Page 155: Photo © 2018 Janet Hall/RIBA Collections | Pages 158–59, 166, 266: Photo © 2018 James Mortimer/World of Interiors | Page 160: Photo © 2018 Horst P. Horst, courtesy of Hamiltons Gallery London | Page 161: Photo © 2018 Julien Nyman/Country Life | Page 162–3: Photo courtesy of Colefax and Fowler | Page 168–69: Photo © 2018 Christopher Simon Sykes/House & Garden/Condé Nast | Page 170: Photo © 2018 David Montgomery/Getty Images | Pages 171, 172–73, 183, 206–7, 238–39: Photos © 2018 Fritz von der Schulenburg/The Interior Archive | Pages 174, 175, 187, 190, 192–93, 238–39, 287: Photos © 2018 Simon Upton/The Interior Archive | Pages 176–177: Photo © Michael Nicholson/World of Interiors | Page 178: Photo © 2018 Steve Pyke/Getty Images | Page 182: Photo © 2018 Simon Brown | Page 184–85: Photo courtesy of Nina Campbell/photography Simon Brown | Pages 186, 303: Photos © 2018 Architectural Digest/Condé Nast | Page 188–89: Photo © 2018 Tessa Traeger | Page 191: Photo © 2018 Lucas Allen/House & Garden/Condé Nast | Pages 194, 195, 196–97: Photo © 2018 Simon Brown/courtesy of Kit Kemp | Pages 198, 199: Photos © 2018 Simon Bevan | Page 200–1: Photo © 2018 Jason Ingram | Pages 208, 210, 211: Photo courtesy of Gourcuff Gradenigo | Page 209: Photo © 2018 Celia Denney | Page 212 (bottom), 248: Photo © 2018 Karen Radkai/Architectural Digest/Condé Nast | Page 213: Photo © 2018 Elizabeth Heyert | Pages 214–15, 292–93, 304–5: Photos © 2018 Michel Arnaud | Page 216 (top): Photo © 2018 Christophe von Hohenberg | Page 217: Photo © 2018 R. Landin/Hatchette | Page 220: Photo © 2018 Alexandre Bailhache | Pages 221, 222–23, 232: Photos © 2018 Francois Halard/Trunk Archive | Page 224: Photo © 2018 Christies | Page 225: Photo © 2018 Marina Faust/Architectural Digest/Condé Nast | Page 228: Photo © 2018 Mark Peterson/Getty Images | Pages 229, 233: Photos © 2018 Lea Crespi | Page 234–35: Photo © 2018 Jacques Denarnaud | Page 237: Photo © 2018 Martino Lombezzi/Contrasto/ Redux | Pages 240, 267: Photos © 2018 Phillip Ennis | Page 241: Photo © 2018 Circe Hamilton | Pages 244, 354 (top): Photo © 2018 Philippe Garcia/Architectural Digest France/Condé Nast | Page 245: Photo © 2018 Antoine Bootz | Pages 246–247: Photo © 2018 Guido Taroni | Page 250–51: Photo © 2018 Neal Slavin | Page 253: Photo © 2018 House & Garden/Condé Nast | Page 254: Photo © 2018 Peter Peirce/Architectural Digest/Condé Nast | Page 255: Photo © 2018 Phil Mansfield | Page 258: Photo © 2018 Nick

Johnson | Pages 260–61, 268–69: Photos © 2018 Scott Frances/Otto | Pages 262, 354, 356–57: Photos © 2018 Bjorn Wallander/Otto | Page 263 (appeared in "Timeless Elegance" by David Easton): Photo © 2018 David O. Marlow | Page 264–65: Photo © 2018 Andrew Shurtleff | Page 271: Photo © 2018 Douglas Friedman/Trunk Archive | Page 274 (top): Photo © 2018 Anton Bruehl/Condé Nast via Getty Images | Pages 274 (bottom), 275: Photos © 2018 Cooper Hewitt, Smithsonian Design Museum / Art Resource, NY | Page 276: Photo © 2018 John Kobal Foundation/Getty Images | Page 277: Photo © 2018 Allan Grant/The LIFE Picture Collection, 1959/Getty | Page 278: Photo © 2018 Mark Davidson | Pages 280, 282–83: Photo © 2018 Tim Street-Porter | Page 281: Photo © 2018 Guy Webster/Uber Archives | Page 286 (top): Photo courtesy of the Palm Springs Historical Society | Page 286 (bottom): Photos © 2018 Fritz Taggart/Architectural Digest/Condé Nast | Page 288: Photo © 2018 Lisl Dennis | Page 289: Photo © 2018 Ivan Terestchenko | Page 291: Photo © 2018 Ira Montgomery/Architectural Digest/Condé Nast | Page 294: Photo © 2018 Alexandre Bailhache | Page 295: Photo © 2018 Luca Trovato | Page 298: Photo © 2018 E. Knoll | Page 297: Photo © 2018 William Abranowicz/Art & Commerce | Page 302: Photo © 2018 Joe Schmelzer | Page 308 (top): Photo courtesy San Diego History Center | Page 309: Photo © 2018 Max Eckhert/Architectural Digest/Condé Nast | Page 310: Photo © 2018 J. Reid/Condé Nast | Pages 312–13, 316–317, 318 (bottom), 320: Photo © 2018 Peter Vitale/Architectural Digest/Condé Nast | Page 314: Photo © 2018 Sheldon Lettich/Architectural Digest/Condé Nast | Page 315: Photo © 2018 John Vaughan/Architectural Digest/Condé Nast | Page 318 (top): Photo © 2018 Harry Benson/Architectural Digest/Condé Nast | Page 321: Photo © 2018 Feliciano/Condé Nast | Page 322: Photo © 2018 John M. Hall | Page 323: Courtesy of Jed Johnson Home | Page 324: Photo © 2018 Mary E. Nicols/Architectural Digest/Condé Nast | Pages 330, 370, 371, 372–73: Photos © 2018 Eric Piasecki/Otto | Page 334: Photo © 2018 Peter Ash Lee/Art & Commerce | Page 339: Interior design by Brian J. McCarthy Inc., photography by Fritz von der Schulenburg | Pages 340–41, 343: Photos © 2018 Max Kim-Bee | Page 342: Photo © 2018 Lisa Romerein/Otto | Page 344–45: Photo © 2018 Amy Neunsinger | Page 346, 348–49: Photo © 2018 Matthieu Salvaing/Otto | Page 347: Photo © 2018 Jason Schmidt | Page 350: Photo © 2018 Caryn B. Davis Photography | Page 351, 352–53: Collection of Bruce Budd, New York | Page 355: Photo © 2018 Photography by Roger Davies, courtesy of Architectural Digest | Page 358 (bottom): Photo © 2018 Stephan Julliard | Pages 359, 360–61: Photos © 2018 Pascal Chevallier | Pages 362, 363: Photo © 2018 Mark Edward Harris | Page 364–65: Courtesy of Kelly Wearstler, photography by Grey Crawford | Page 367: Courtesy of Markham Roberts | Page 368–69: Photo © 2018 Nelson Hancock | Pages 374, 375, 376–77: Photos © 2018 Melanie Acevedo | Pages 378, 379, 380–81: Photos © 2018 Scott Frances/Otto | Page 382: Photo © 2018 Mark C. O'Flaherty | Page 383: Photo © 2018 Xavier Bejot | Page 384–85: Photo © 2018 Stephan Julliard/Tripod Agency

Best efforts were made to verify all photo credits. Any oversight was unintentional and should be brought to the publisher's attention so that it can be corrected in a future printing.

INSPIRED DESIGN
First published in 2018 by The Vendome Press
Vendome is a registered trademark of The Vendome Press, LLC

NEW YORK
Suite 2043
244 Fifth Avenue
New York, NY 10001
www.vendomepress.com

LONDON
63 Edith Grove
London,
SW10 0LB, UK
www.vendomepress.co.uk

Copyright © 2018 The Vendome Press
Text © 2018 Jennifer Boles

Distributed in North America by Abrams Books
Distributed in the United Kingdom, and the rest of the world, by Thames & Hudson

ISBN 978-0-86565-356-6

PUBLISHERS: Beatrice Vincenzini, Mark Magowan, and Francesco Venturi
EDITOR: Stephen Drucker
PRODUCTION DIRECTOR: Jim Spivey
DESIGNER: Celia Fuller
PHOTO RESEARCHER: Vivien Hamley

Library of Congress Cataloging-in-Publication Data available upon request.

Printed and bound in China by 1010 Printing International Ltd.

FIRST PRINTING

Page ii In the 1970s, California designer Michael Taylor created a revolutionary design style that dramatized natural elements.

Page vi Hadley's restrained approach to design was best seen in his own enormously chic Manhattan living room. He once quipped, "Some people can't live without whoopsy curtains—I can't live with them."

Page 1 "Cliffoney" fabric in Gold/Mink, from the David Hicks by Ashley Hicks collection. Courtesy of Lee Jofa.

Page 33 "Poetic Plush" fabric in Cumin, designed by Barbara Barry. Courtesy of Kravet.

Page 77 Textile wallpaper designed by Beaudesert Limited incorporating sketches by Sir Cecil Beaton of high society figures of 1929.

Page 99 "Lyford Trellis" wallpaper in Natural on Brown on Cream. Courtesy of Quadrille.

Page 149 "Rick Rack" fabric in Orange, designed by Kit Kemp. Courtesy of Christopher Farr.

Page 201 "Marais Stripe" fabric in Cordovan. Courtesy of Kravet.

Page 241 "Le Leopard" fabric in Sable. Courtesy of Lee Jofa.

Page 271 "Rhododendron" wallpaper in Cream. Courtesy of Carleton V.

Page 305 "Foliage" fabric in Beige. Courtesy of Jed Johnson Home.

Page 327 "Chalet" wallpaper in Ivory/Gold, designed by Kelly Wearstler. Courtesy of Lee Jofa.